THEY'VE
CROSSED
THE LINE

A PATRIOT'S GUIDE TO
RELIGIOUS
FREEDOM

Foreword by Senator Rick Santorum

THEY'VE
CROSSED
THE LINE

A PATRIOT'S GUIDE TO
RELIGIOUS
FREEDOM

STEPHEN
BLOOM

KERRIÉL
BAILEY

GOD & COUNTRY
PRESS

They've Crossed the Line:
A Patriot's Guide to Religious Freedom

First Printing—January, 2013

Print edition	ISBN 13: 978-0-89957-166-9
EPUB edition	ISBN 13: 978-1-61715-298-6
Mobi edition	ISBN 13: 978-1-61715-299-3
ePDF edition	ISBN 13: 978-1-61715-300-6

Cover layout and design by Michael Largent
at InView Graphics, Chattanooga, TN

Interior design and typesetting by
Adept Content Solutions LLC,
Urbana, IL

Editing by Stephen and Amanda Sorenson and Rick Steele

Printed in Canada
18 17 16 15 14 13 –MAR– 6 5 4 3 2 1

Also by Stephen Bloom:

The Believers Guide to Legal Issues
(Living Ink Books)

Table of Contents

At School ———————————————————— ☆

At Work ———————————————————— ☆

And Everywhere Else ——————————☆

Acknowledgments ✧

Stephen:

With deepest gratitude to Dan Penwell (1942-2010), the editor who so graciously plucked me out of the literary slush-pile and changed my life forever, and who was so remarkably supportive of this, my second project, from the moment we shared the idea. It was a high privilege to work with you, Brother.

Also, thanks to Rick Steele and the whole AMG/God & Country Press team for so ably seeing the project through. And to Stephen and Amanda Sorenson for your most skillful and perceptive copyediting.

To Josh Autry, Esq., thanks for your expertise in helping to identify and organize the pressing issues of religious liberty, and to Christie McGinley, thanks for your thorough research into the magnitude of the threats to that liberty.

And to my co-author, Kerriél Bailey, thanks for your enthusiasm in tackling this project, and for your perserverence though the challenging circumstances you overcame.

To my lovely wife, Sharon, you are so appreciated and so gifted at setting others up for success.

And lastly, thank you to our Founding Fathers, whose faith, courage and wisdom stoked the flames of American religious freedom which still burn so brightly.

Kerriél:

My heart-felt gratitude to my co-author Stephen Bloom for giving me the opportunity to write with him on a subject so near and dear to my heart.

Thank you Rick Steele and AMG/God & Country Press for being so patient and gracious in spite of many delays and obstacles in bringing this project to fruition.

To the amazing constitutional scholars from the American Center for Law & Justice and Alliance Defending Freedom (formerly Alliance Defense Fund) and the Christian Legal Society Center for Law and Religious Freedom whom I have had the privilege to work with and learn from over the years.

Thank you to my wonderful friends and family who prayed me through this project. And my particularly my best friend and husband Kurt who has always encouraged me to follow my dreams as I seek to serve the Lord in the field of law.

Foreword ✫ Rick Santorum, United States Senator (Pennsylvania), 1995-2007

I s it still safe to live out our Christian faith in an increasingly secularized and hostile society? Do we risk being punished at school or on the job if we dare to take a stand for Christ? Can we be forced to shut up and sit down when we try to speak for Jesus in the public square? What are our legal rights as American Christians in post-Christian America?

Stephen Bloom and Kerriel Bailey's book, *They've Crossed the Line: A Patriot's Guide to Religious Freedom,* provides concise easy-to-understand legal answers for the everyday religious freedom questions Christians face in their lives and communities. And there's good news! In most cases, the law says, "Yes, you still have the right to be a Christian at school, at work, and everywhere else!"

Each chapter begins with a short fictional vignette drawn from real-life controversies and circumstances. The stories are engaging, but intentionally unresolved, setting the stage for the legal counsel to follow. The tone of the counsel is simple and direct, to connect with the non-attorney readers for whom the book is written. The relevant concepts are boiled down to plain English.

Mr. Bloom and Mrs. Bailey are legal scholars in the tradition of our founding fathers. Our nation's founders knew the essential importance of religious liberty. The American

Revolution was as much about liberty as it was about taxation. In 18th Century America the term "pursuit of happiness" meant the pursuit of the morally right. The free exercise of religion is that pursuit of happiness.

Readers of this book will be encouraged and empowered to engage the culture as bold witnesses for their faith. The book will embolden believers to break free from the false constraints of prevailing misconceptions. Misconceptions popularized and perpetuated by the anti-Christian secular Left and its allies in law, media, education, and entertainment that Christians are legally relegated to the status of passive observers on the sidelines of American life. People of faith aren't just *allowed* to participate vigorously in the public arena of our democracy, they are *called* to do so. Bloom and Bailey's book will give them a clear path to participation.

Senator Rick Santorum
patriotvoices.com

They've Crossed the Line...

At School

Remove Your Shirt!
Clothing, Words, and Symbols of Faith

Prayer-Free Zones?
Prayer in the Classroom, Locker Room,
on the Playground...

You Can't Have That Book in Here!
Bibles and Bible Clubs

**Excuse Me, You Want My Child to
Write About What?**
Assignments vs. Conscience

**Shush Children,
No Talking About God!**
Witnessing at School

1

Chapter 1

Remove Your Shirt! Clothing, Words, and Symbols of Faith

Kamerin was awake when her alarm clock went off. Remembering her mother's suggestion, she prayed, "God, please help me to be calm today, my first day at high school." Yet her mind raced, flooding with fearful thoughts. *I wish I could just stay at middle school. I'll have to ride a bus, use a locker, buy lunch in a giant cafeteria, go to so many classes, meet strange kids from other schools.... Will I get lost? Will I make friends? Will I find my bus after school?*

When Mom walked in carrying a basket of clean clothes, Kamerin turned away, hiding her tear-stained face in the pillow. "Another minute, Kam, and you need to be downstairs for breakfast," Mom said firmly. The thought of eating made Kamerin queasy, but she was thirsty. She felt shaky as she climbed out of bed.

Glancing at the laundry basket, Kamerin smiled. Her freshly washed, summer-camp tee shirt lay on top of the pile, neatly folded. She pressed the shirt to her face, smelling a faint scent of pine and campfire smoke deep in the soft cotton. Scenes of sitting around the campfire during the last night of camp, only a week ago, flashed into her mind. *I'll never forget that night,* she reflected, her heart strangely warmed—*when God deeply stirred my heart, when I experienced his love for me like never before and joyfully gave my life to Jesus Christ.*

As she put on the tee shirt, her anxieties about high school started slipping away, and the peace she experienced that night at camp returned. *Everything will be okay.* She looked in a mirror on the way downstairs, happy to see the bold camp logo on her shirt--mountains with a rising cross. It reminded her of Hebrews 11:1, the Bible verse printed on the back of her shirt, the one that all the campers memorized: "Now faith is being sure of what we hope for and certain of what we do not see."

The bus arrived on time, and her first two classes went well. As her third class began, Kamerin was feeling good. *Everything has been awesome so far—the bus ride, locker details, the other kids. I haven't even gotten lost yet!* Of course she still wondered how and where she'd fit in with other girls representing so many different cultures and backgrounds. Even the diversity of clothing styles amazed Kamerin. Some kids dressed like celebrities; others appeared dangerous and rebellious. *I'll just try to be myself,* she pondered. *Mom would never approve of the fashions some of these girls are wearing. I'll stick with my tee shirt and jeans.*

As Kamerin listened to the teacher, she daydreamed about an optimistic strategy for lunch, her last big challenge of this day. *I know a few girls from middle school, and Emma—from church. When the bell rings, I'll stick tightly with those girls, and we'll work our way through the cafeteria maze and sit as a group. That way, none of us will face the dreadful embarrassment of eating alone.*

Suddenly this announcement rang out over the classroom public address system: "Kamerin Miller, report to the principal's office. Kamerin Miller, to the principal's office." Kamerin sensed every eye focusing on her. Her neck felt hot and red. Sweating, she sat paralyzed at the unwanted attention as a mocking chorus of "wooo-oooh!" filled the room. Finally the teacher silenced the students and, apparently blaming

Kamerin for the disruption, snapped harshly, "Well, don't just sit there, Kamerin, go!"

Her heart pounding, Kamerin tried to find the principal's office. *Why me? I've never been in trouble at school.* Panicked thoughts jumbled her mind as she realized something terrible might have happened. *Has Mom been hurt in a car crash, ...or worse?* Tears welling up, sobbing, she entered the school offices.

A school secretary gave Kamerin a harsh stare, shook her head disapprovingly, and then pointed to an inner office. Kamerin timidly stepped into the cramped room. She recognized the principal who spoke during the opening assembly that morning, then noticed a female nurse and a male security guard. *Mom's dead,* she thought, trying to be brave as all three adults sat and stared. Then the principal said, "Kamerin, you need to remove your shirt."

"Wait, what?" she stammered, puzzled and bewildered.

The principal repeated his words: "Kamerin, you need to remove your shirt."

Kamerin's head spun; she couldn't catch her breath. "Remove my shirt?" she gasped in disbelief. "No!" Trembling and confused, she turned to leave, but the guard commanded her to remain in the room.

The principal shouted angrily, "You're in violation of the student dress code, young lady. The proselytizing message on your shirt is disruptive to the classroom environment, and its blatant religious symbolism is offensive to our academic community's values. We have zero tolerance for this type of intentional disrespect for the rights of other students."

The principal kept talking, but Kamerin—tears streaming down her face—had no idea what he meant. Finally he said, "Miss Ross, our school nurse, will assist you in changing clothes." He and the guard then left the room and closed the door.

"Remove your shirt," the nurse commanded.

Disoriented but relieved the men were gone, Kamerin complied reluctantly. The nurse took the tee shirt and handed her a grubby, pink-hooded sweatshirt big enough for even the largest dress-code violators. It hung on Kamerin like an oversized tent as she watched helplessly as the nurse wadded up her beloved tee shirt and stuffed it into a plastic grocery bag. "The principal will maintain custody of this shirt until your parent or guardian arranges to retrieve it," the nurse explained, "You can make one phone call from the office to ask someone to bring you a suitable replacement shirt today. Otherwise, wear this sweatshirt home, and bring it back to your homeroom teacher tomorrow, washed and dried."

The nurse led Kamerin back to the secretary's desk, and the secretary shoved an unfamiliar phone in her direction. With unsteady fingers, Kamerin dialed her mother's number but the call went straight to voice mail. Self conscious and unsure how to explain her plight, Kamerin hung up without leaving a message. The secretary shrugged, pulled the phone back to her side of the desk, pointed at her wristwatch, and motioned Kamerin toward the cafeteria down the hall.

Kamerin desperately hoped to slip into the cafeteria unnoticed and find her acquaintances. She didn't even care about eating now. But she recognized no one in the huge, crowded room. Boys burst into mocking laughter as she wandered around in the pink sweatshirt. Soon everyone was pointing and laughing. Kamerin, humiliated and alone, ran out of the cafeteria and slumped in the hallway outside the door until it was time for students to go to their afternoon classes. Acutely aware of her classmates' burning stares, Kamerin sat downcast through her remaining classes and was the first student to get on the bus.

Kamerin and her mother talked, hugged, and prayed for hours that evening. After all the tears, they read Bible passages about faithful followers of God being killed or suffering terrible harm because of their faith. So many original disciples of Christ suffered and died for their faith, and so many of them suffer and are killed today. When Kamerin compared their torture and death with having her favorite shirt confiscated and being laughed at by fellow students, her experiences didn't seem so bad after all!

The powerful peace she first experienced by the fire at camp returned, stronger than ever, as if God were saying, "Yes, sometimes you will be laughed at because you believe in me. Maybe you will even be hurt or killed because you believe in me. But be strong and courageous because I will always be with you. I will always love you."

As Kamerin drifted off to sleep with a gentle smile on her lips, her mother thanked God for the wisdom he had provided to help guide and calm her daughter after such a tough day. She then prayerfully reflected on what to do next. *Was it really legal for the school to take away Kamerin's shirt just because it had a cross and Bible verse on it? Are Christian kids really restricted from displaying their faith in school? Is Kamerin being called to serve God in a way bigger than either of us can imagine? Is this the moment we are supposed to take our stand, to honor Jesus Christ and all those who died and suffered for him? Tomorrow I will contact a good lawyer about this situation.*

Counsel for Christians

There is widespread confusion about students' legal rights to express their religious faith freely in the public school environment. Some teachers, administrators, and parents seem determined to prevent students from showing even the slightest evidence of Christian belief at school. Their reasons may be as simple as innocent confusion about the law or as complex as strategic anti-Christian agendas. Either way, school officials everywhere are going out of their way to shut down any sort of religious expression by students at school. The unfortunate result? Many students' basic constitutional rights are violated.

More than forty years ago, in the 1969 case of *Tinker vs. Des Moines Independent Community School District,* the Supreme Court of the United States powerfully declared that neither students nor teachers "shed their constitutional rights ... at the schoolhouse gate."[1] This decision confirmed a long history of similar rulings that Supreme Court Justices called "the unmistakable holding of this Court for almost 50 years."[2] These cases, which recognize and protect the religious liberties of students at school, remain the law of our land today. Amazingly, many school leaders still find themselves immersed in legal misinformation and false ideas about their students' constitutionally granted religious freedoms.

Free speech is a fundamental right of students, including those attending public schools. The First Amendment of the United States Constitution assures that all Americans are guaranteed the right to freedom of speech, and that free speech can be more than just spoken words. Free speech includes other expressive activity such as wearing religious symbols or religious messages on tee shirts. Students don't lose their right to express their opinions or beliefs just because they attend public schools.

The right we all have to express ourselves freely is a core American value guaranteed in our Constitution. A student has this right "in the cafeteria, or on the playing field, or on the campus,"[3] according to the Supreme Court, and in all these places "he may express his opinions."[4] Despite the fact

---

1   *Tinker v. Des Moines Independent Community School District,* 393 U.S. 503, 506 (1969).

2   Ibid.

3   Id at 512-513.

4   Id.

that Supreme Court decisions are binding on all federal and state courts throughout our nation, many school officials still wrongly believe they can arbitrarily restrict the expressive religious speech of students.

School dress codes governing student clothing and other apparel are considered legally permissible only if such codes are religiously neutral and apply to everyone. Although most of us probably don't want students bombarded with vulgar or indecent messages that might appear on student clothing in the absence of school dress codes, all dress codes must be designed to respect students' constitutional rights on the public school campus.

So, if a school dress code allows students to wear tee shirts with slogans (such as advertisements or messages of any kind), the school can't deny a student such as Kamerin the right to wear a tee shirt communicating a Christian message. Student speech expressed through clothing and accessories can't be restricted because of the content of the message unless it is vulgar or somehow "materially and substantially"[5] interferes with school discipline.

For example, if a school prohibits profanity on clothing, a Christian student can't expect to be allowed to wear a shirt with the word "hell" on it, even though the context of the message is religious rather than profane. Under the law, banning the shirt would be considered a legally acceptable, neutral rule that applies to everyone. There is generally no religious exception from anti-profanity rules in a school dress code.

What about the legal rule that school officials can limit students' rights to express free speech when exercise of these rights materially and substantially interferes with school discipline? The free speech in question must *actually* cause interference with the school's operation. A mere fear, belief, or concern about interference isn't enough.

---

5   Ibid.

In 1969, students involved in the *Tinker* case wore black armbands to protest the Vietnam War. The Supreme Court said that "the wearing of armbands in the circumstances of this case was entirely divorced from actually or potentially disruptive conduct from those participating in it."[6] Students' speech cannot be stifled simply because they express a view different from the school administration.

There is also no constitutional right *not* to be offended. The school officials involved in the *Tinker* case attempted to punish students for nonverbal, passive expression of a viewpoint, much like when school officials attempt to censor students for wearing tee shirts conveying a Christian message. The Court prohibited this kind of censorship. The Court said that the school's action in punishing students who wore armbands amounted to punishing speech because it *might* instigate a debate or *might* trigger arguments among students who disagree with the message. "Might" is not a good enough legal reason to trample on the Constitution!

It's important for us to understand, though, that not all categories of speech are treated the same under the law. Things do get a little tricky. Everyone knows you can't yell "Fire" in a crowded theater even though the Constitution guarantees your right to free speech. Likewise, some forms of student speech *can* be restricted.

In another Supreme Court case, *Bethel School District vs. Fraser*[7], the Court found that offensively lewd and indecent speech was "low-value" speech in schools and did not enjoy the same protection under the First Amendment as other speech. The Court made the same ruling in the case of *Morse vs. Frederick*[8], upholding student discipline after students displayed a banner promoting illegal drug use because that prohibition

---

6   Ibid, 516.

7   478 U.S. 675 (1986).

8   551 U.S. 393 (2007).

on speech was an acceptable restriction of the First Amendment in the school setting. Just because low-value student speech can be lawfully restricted, however, doesn't mean in most cases and places that schools can restrict high-value religious, political, or unpopular student speech.

Unfortunately, expression of student speech on the topic of homosexuality *can* currently be restricted in certain western states (Alaska, Arizona, California, Hawaii, Idaho, Montana, Nevada, Oregon, and Washington) and Pacific territories according to a much-criticized United States Court of Appeals, Ninth Circuit case, *Harper v. Poway Unified School District*.[9] In that case, a school's ban of a student's tee-shirt message opposing homosexuality was upheld even though the message was religious. The court said that such speech "collides with the rights of other students." This unusual legal standard seems blatantly contrary to our Constitution, but unless and until the Supreme Court decides otherwise, there are different rules on schools restricting speech on homosexuality depending on where you live!

Quick Counsel for Christians

★ Students have constitutional rights to free speech, even on a public school campus.

★ Students can freely express religious beliefs at school through words, clothing, and symbols.

★ When there's a school dress code, students can wear religious messages if the code allows other kinds of messages.

☆ Note: Anti-homosexual messages can be restricted in certain western states and Pacific territories.

---

9   485 F.3d 1052 (9th Cir., 2007).

★ A school can't restrict a student's religious expression because of a mere fear, belief, or concern.

★ A school can't restrict a student's religious expression unless such a decision is based on *actual* "material and substantial" disruption of school discipline.

★ A school can restrict a student's expression of low-value speech, such as vulgarity.

Chapter 2

Prayer-Free Zones? Prayer in the Classroom, Locker Room, on the Playground...

Corky always had to be the center of attention at Lee Elementary School. Fun loving, athletic, and fearless, he especially loved to captivate his third-grade classmates with daring feats and risky antics during recess. If he often ended up with extra scrapes and bruises, that was okay with him. It just added to his rough-and-tumble, daredevil reputation.

When Corky happened to watch a television show one evening featuring urban climbers who scale the vertical exterior walls of skyscrapers, he instantly planned his ascent of his two-story school building. The next morning, he boasted to all his friends in class about how he would climb up to the roof during recess. And when recess began, Corky didn't disappoint the small crowd of kids who gathered in a partially hidden spot alongside the building's vertical face to behold his latest triumph.

Corky knew how engage his audience with drama. He began by explaining and briefly demonstrating his climbing technique, emphasizing the immense physical strength and concentration necessary for success. Then he previewed his carefully selected route, highlighting the most dangerous and challenging obstacles to a successful climb. Finally, he reminded his peers of the terrible risks involved.

First, there was the risk of getting caught by a teacher, which might mean his suspension or even expulsion from school. Second there was the risk of falling, which he assured everyone would mean death or, at the very least, paralysis. To drive his point home, Corky slapped his hand hard on the unforgiving concrete sidewalk. Third, there was the peculiar risk that he might be permanently trapped on the school roof should he succeed with the climb, leaving himself with the fearful choice of either jumping or starving. By the time Corky was ready to proceed with his adventure, the small audience understood that the stakes were high indeed.

Finally it was time for Corky to climb. Within seconds, he was skillfully scampering up the side of the building, clinging with fingertips and sneaker toes to the tiniest seams and ledges. He expertly overcame the most difficult challenges along his planned course. At last, as he neared the roofline, he grabbed hold of a metal rain gutter and began pulling himself toward his final goal. A brief smile of satisfaction crossed his face. The kids below gazed in awe. Then the gutter gave way, snapping off in Corky's hands.

Corky landed fast and hard, crumpling into an awkward heap. The terrified third-graders immediately knew Corky was hurt badly. His body shook and shuddered as scarlet blood oozed through his blond hair onto the concrete. His eyes were bulging. His mouth was moving, but no words came out.

Zack, one of Corky's classmates and his best friend since kindergarten, ran as fast as he could to get help from the teacher doing recess monitor duty. Zack practically dragged and tugged the teacher all the way back to the spot of the fall, trying to make her comprehend the extreme urgency. When she finally saw Corky's condition, she thanked Zack and frantically dialed 911 and then the school nurse.

As Zack watched and worried about Corky, he wondered, *Is he paralyzed? Will he die?* Desiring to do something to help, Zack remembered something his grandfather, a preacher, had emphasized over and over since he was little.

"Zack, don't forget to pray—it's something anyone can do, and God always hears."

The other kids stood there in shock, some of them crying. The teacher, overwhelmed and desperately awaiting emergency help, tried to comfort Corky. Zack, suddenly emboldened, blurted out his grandfather's advice, "Let's pray –it's something anyone can do, and God always hears!" Then Zack bowed his head and started praying, just like he had always seen his grandfather do in church and at family gatherings, loudly and clearly. "Lord Jesus, we pray for Corky, we pray for you to heal him, we pray for you to let him live, we pray for Corky's mom, we pray for Corky's dad, we pray for the ambulance driver, we pray for the nurse... ." As Zack prayed, the other kids closed their eyes and bowed their heads, too.

A few moments later, the school nurse and principal breathlessly arrived on the scene. While the nurse cared for Corky and the ambulance siren grew louder, the principal— surprised to encounter the praying students—tapped Zack on the shoulder and whispered, "You can't pray here, this is public school property."

Zack, having been taught by his parents to respect his teachers and principal, immediately ended his prayer with a quick "amen" and then apologized to the principal. "I didn't know praying was against the rules." The principal just mumbled something to Zack about "not letting it happen again." Zack thought about asking why praying wasn't allowed at school, but by then the principal was yelling into his cell phone and directing his office assistant to notify Corky's family of the grave medical situation.

The sound of sirens soon filled the air. Other teachers rushed onto the playground to gather up the children, including Zack. During the rest of the school day, everyone in Zack's class worried about Corky whenever they glanced at his empty seat. Finally, just before the last bell for dismissal, the teacher announced that Corky had suffered a mild concussion and had several broken bones, but was expected to make a full recovery. Zack smiled and silently thanked God for answering his prayers.

News and rumors of Corky's climb and terrible fall swept through the small town. Even the local television and radio stations covered the story, with live reports from the school and hospital as well as interviews with school administrators and Corky's family members. One station interviewed an expert rock climbing instructor who evaluated the degree of difficulty of Corky's route.

At dinner that night, Zack's parents asked him how he was feeling and listened to his eyewitness account of Corky's climb and fall. As they ate Zack's favorite home-cooked meal—hot dogs, macaroni and cheese, and applesauce—he told the whole story, step by step.

After outlining the technical intricacies and mechanics of Corky's climb, the sudden shock of his fall, and details of his injuries, Zack proudly explained that he was the first kid to run and get help. He expected to receive generous praises. Instead, his parents launched into a stern lecture on why he should have reported Corky's planned climb to a teacher before it happened instead of waiting until Corky was nearly killed. "You failed to take personal responsibility," his father stated.

As Zack grudgingly accepted the lessons his parents were trying to instill, he wondered if he should even tell them about the prayer he led for Corky and how the principal scolded him for praying. Sensing another lecture coming, and believing that honesty would be the best policy, he went ahead and told his parents that part of the story, too.

After Zack finished speaking, his father thought for a moment and said, "Zack, Grandpa would sure be proud of you for praying like that, but you really ought to know better than to pray at school. Everybody knows praying in school is against the rules."

Zack's mom nodded her head. "Yes, you should know better, Zack. At least you didn't get detention or other punishment. Most importantly, Corky is going to be okay. Let's visit him in the hospital as soon as he can have visitors. And from now on, pray for him when you are home, not at school!"

Well, that wasn't too bad, as lectures go, Zack thought, *but I wonder why I can't pray at school? It doesn't hurt anyone, and Grandpa says it helps. I think schools would want us kids to be praying. I just don't get it. Maybe I'll understand when I'm older.*

"Yeah, Mom, let's visit Corky soon," Zack replied, "and I'll keep praying for him when I'm not at school. Oh, can you please pass me more applesauce?"

Counsel for Christians

The good news is that prayer in public school is constitutionally protected! In fact, the Supreme Court explicitly said so in *Santa Fe Independent School District v. Doe.*[10] The Court held that "nothing in the Constitution...prohibits any public school student from voluntarily praying at any time before, during, or after the school day." Yet many school officials and parents alike are confused about this issue.

The First Amendment of the Constitution protects the rights of speech and expression, as well as religion. This includes elementary, middle school, and high school students. The Supreme Court clearly holds that "private religious speech, far from being a First Amendment orphan, is as fully protected under the Free Speech Clause as secular private expression" (*Capital Square Review & Advisory Board v. Pinette*).[11]

---

10 Santa Fe Independent School District v. Doe, 530 U.S. 290 (2000).
11 Capital Square Review & Advisory Board v. Pinette, 515 U.S. 753, 760 (1995).

The First Amendment provides freedom to express religious views and protects students from a school official meddling in their religious expression and activities. But that right is not without limits. It is subject to the same conditions and rules of order that govern other student speech. For example, if children are allowed to talk to each other during recess, then they can also pray during recess—not just alone but with other students, too. Certainly students cannot force or coerce other students to participate in group prayer, but they can extend an offer to pray for a classmate. If students are allowed in a particular area of the school, they can pray while they are there. The playground during recess is no exception.

If students have quiet times during school when they can quietly talk to one another, then they can quietly pray with one another, too. If students are permitted to talk to one another in the hallways or the cafeteria, then those places are also open for prayer. Students can certainly pray with other students just as they can talk with other students!

Public school officials must be neutral regarding religious activity initiated by students, meaning there can be no discrimination or favoritism. For example, a time cannot be set aside for religion, nor can students be prohibited from praying during periods set aside for free time. The Supreme Court, in *Rosenberger v. Rector and Visitors of the University of Virginia*[12], tells us that the Constitution mandates neutrality rather than hostility toward privately initiated religious expression.

What about praying in the locker room before a game? If students are free to talk to one another, then they can also pray with each other as long as it is student led and student initiated. According to legal precedent, such locker room prayer runs afoul of the Constitution only if it is sanctioned

------

12 515 U.S. 819 (1995).

by a coach or other school official. The Supreme Court said in *Sante Fe* that not every message delivered on school property is government speech, likewise private student speech in a locker room.

Not only can students pray in public school, but schools must certify in writing each year that they do not have any policy that "prevents or otherwise denies participation in constitutionally protected prayer in public elementary and secondary schools." And their funding may depend on it! In order for a school to receive federal funding under the Elementary and Secondary Education Act (ESEA), a local educational agency must certify in writing each year that there is no such policy impinging on a student's constitutional right to pray. Section 9254 of the ESEA states that local educational agencies, such as public schools and school districts, must not certify in bad faith either. So, if a school certifies it is in compliance but actually has a policy that prevents or otherwise denies participation in prayer, the school is subject to enforcement action. That enforcement action can include withholding of federal funding until the policy is brought into alignment with the Constitution. The U.S. Department of Education requires state departments of education to review and respond to citizens' complaints about schools that do not follow the guidelines. How many public school officials might get their policies in line with the Constitution if they knew their school's funding depended on it?

The ESEA also requires the secretary of education to issue "guidance" to help state and local educational agencies and the public understand constitutionally protected prayer in public elementary and secondary schools. The U.S. Department of Education issued guidance in 2003 and confirmed it as recently as November 22, 2011. The guidance explains that the First Amendment to the Constitution protects student speech—religious speech as well as political and personal speech.

Not only can students pray aloud in public school, they can pray silently, too. For example, students are free to pray at mealtimes. Just because children attend a public school does not mean that they must refrain from mealtime prayer! Likewise, if a school has a "moment of silence" or other quiet time during the school day, a student can use that time to pray. Sometimes elementary school students can go to a quiet reading area in their classrooms if they finish a project or assignment before the rest of their classmates. Such a quiet area would be a permissible place for a child to pray.

"As long as there are tests," a saying states, "there will be prayer in school." This is another example of a constitutionally permissible type of prayer allowed in public school. Students can pray before a test just as students can participate in a relaxation exercise prior to taking a test.

Students can lead organized prayer groups like "See You at the Pole" , an event that takes place on the fourth Wednesday in September each year. This event sets aside a time when students meet at the flagpole in front of their respective schools for a time of prayer. Millions of students gather each year in all fifty states and some twenty countries. To pass judicial muster, these types of group events must be student led and student initiated, however. Such gatherings are perfectly lawful just like other nonreligious gatherings. For example, if students are permitted to organize before school to show support for a child with cancer, they can do so for religious causes, including prayer. Remember, the key is that the conduct cannot "materially or substantially interfere with school discipline."

Another issue of public school prayer arises when a student selected as valedictorian gives a religious speech at graduation. This issue remains contentious and is frequently litigated. The U.S. Department of Education, in its guidance concerning prayer in public schools, indicates that when students or graduation speakers are selected on the basis of "genuinely neutral, evenhanded criteria," and as long as the individual speakers control the content of their own speeches, such speeches are not considered to be government speech. Therefore such speeches cannot be restricted because of either religious or nonreligious content. An example of neutral criteria would be the grade point average. If the student with the highest grade point average receives the opportunity to give the graduation speech and is allowed to write his or her own speech, then the school cannot discriminate if the student has religious references in it. Remember, the Supreme Court has made it clear (*Board of Education v. Mergens*) that "there is a crucial difference between government speech endorsing religion, which the Establishment Clause forbids, and private speech endorsing religion, which the Free Speech and Free Exercise Clauses protect."[13]

The bottom line is that public school rules have their place, but they do not trump constitutional rules against religious discrimination. In *Shelton v. Tucker Carr*, the Supreme Court said that "the vigilant protection of constitutional freedoms is nowhere more vital than in the community of American Schools."[14]

Quick Counsel for Christians

★ Students have constitutional rights to pray, even on a public school campus.

★ Students can pray during such free times as recess or lunch.

★ Public schools can't have policies that prevent or otherwise deny participation in student prayer.

---

13 Board of Education of Westside Community Schools v. Mergens, 496 U.S. 226 (1990).

14 Shelton v. Tucker Carr, 364 U.S. 479, 487 (1960).

★ Schools must be neutral regarding student-initiated religious expression, neither favoring it nor discriminating against it.

★ Students can pray with each other, just like they can talk to each other, during noninstructional time.

★ Prayer gatherings such as "See You at the Pole" events are protected if other noncurricular activities are allowed on the school campus.

Chapter 3

You Can't Have *That* Book in Here! Bibles and Bible Clubs

I don't know you that well yet, God, Christina prayed silently as she perched on the edge of a lonely folding chair in the empty school hallway, *but I can already see you have a strange sense of humor! After all the things I've done wrong, all the trouble I've gotten into here at Rivercrest High, who could've guessed I might be getting thrown out of school for reading the Bible! YOUR Bible, God, let me remind you! And in my senior year, just when I'm finally getting my life together and will get my diploma! So, I hope you'll help me in this appeal hearing today because this is my last chance, and it was you and your book that got me into this mess!*

As Christina finished praying, the door to the school conference room clicked open and a frumpy-looking woman wearing outdated clothes motioned to her, stating without introduction, "Ms. Belle, you may now enter. The hearing will commence." Christina stepped hesitantly into the room, nearly tripping in her borrowed high heels. The woman pointed impatiently to the far side of a large table, and Christina quickly sat down, glad that the three members of the Appeals Council scrutinizing her from their seats across the table could not see her trembling knees. The woman then planted herself at the end of the table behind a messy stack of folders and a placard that read, "Legal Counsel."

The members of the Appeals Council each stated their names, the elderly man in the middle identifying himself as the chairman. Skipping over small talk or pleasantries, he abruptly announced, "This is the hearing of the Appeals Council of the River Regional School District on the matter of the expulsion of Christina Belle. Legal Counsel will proceed with the summary of admissible infractions and applicable legal standards."

Christina wished she could have afforded a lawyer, too, but as an eighteen-year-old student living on her own and working part time to pay the rent, that simply wasn't possible. Her skin flushed with embarrassment as the lawyer began a long, monotonous recital of her most serious transgressions at Rivercrest.

"Grade nine," the woman droned, "suspension, in-school, tobacco policy violation; suspension, in-school, fighting. Grade ten: suspension, in-school, truancy; suspension, in-school, drug and alcohol policy violation; suspension, out-of-school, dress code policy violation; suspension, in-school, leaving school premises. Grade eleven: suspension, out-of-school, dress code policy violation; suspension, in-school, drug and alcohol policy violation; suspension, out-of-school, weapons policy violation.

Giving Christina a brief, self-satisfied smirk, the woman continued reading, "The Appeals Council members will note that the record thus establishes nine admissible infractions prior to the current academic year. As the Student Conduct Guidelines clearly state, a student accumulating ten admissible infractions at Rivercrest High shall be subject to expulsion. Now in grade twelve, Ms. Belle has recently committed her tenth admissible infraction, a violation of the community inclusivity policy. This infraction resulted in immediate suspension, out of school, and triggers automatic expulsion. The sole legal issue to be reviewed by the council today is whether the tenth admissible infraction was properly imposed in accordance with the Student Conduct Guidelines. If so, then the process of expulsion will be duly completed forthwith. If not, then Ms. Belle may remain in school, pending any subsequent admissible infraction. The Council is further advised that the sworn affidavit of the instructor who witnessed the infraction in question has been appended to the record and is legally presumed to adequately establish that the infraction did, in fact, occur. Ms. Belle will now submit to interrogation and may offer any testimony or other evidence that she asserts would overcome this presumption."

Christina didn't really understand all the legal jargon, but she understood the rule: ten suspensions and you are expelled. It was embarrassing for her to listen to the long list of all the trouble she'd caused at Rivercrest High, but not because she believed she was innocent of any of it. She had done every single thing she got punished for, plus a lot more that she never got caught doing. Finally, though, she had turned her life around.

"Please rise for interrogation, Ms. Belle," the chairman barked as soon as the legal summary concluded. Christina wanted to cry. Her heart was pounding, her knees visibly shaking. She tried to keep herself together, grasping her small Bible tightly for comfort. She could feel the condemnation of the council members as they stared her down with condescending looks.

"Ms. Belle, isn't it true that you had in your possession during school hours a Christian Bible, and that you openly and without sensitivity to the beliefs of other students and members of our academic community read from that Bible during a supervised study hall?" the chairman accused. "And isn't it true that you defiantly refused to cease and desist from such behavior when a member of our teaching staff directly instructed you to do so?"

"Umm..., I..., well...," Christina began haltingly, "I don't really know about all those big words you just said. If you are asking me, 'Did I have my Bible in study hall? Did I read my Bible in study hall? Did I refuse to put my Bible away?' then the answer is *yes*. I did all those things."

Arching his eyebrows, the chairman glanced at the lawyer and the other two council members. They all nodded at each other, and the chairman said, "Then that concludes my interrogation. Do you have anything else you wish to say, Ms. Belle, before we close the record?"

Christina took a deep breath and began to speak, gaining confidence as she spoke. "Look, you guys know I was trouble; everyone knows I was trouble. I did all those bad things you said. I can make excuses—my mom was sick, my dad was in jail—but those are just excuses. Bottom line is I used a lot of people, and I let a lot of people use me. You don't know half the stuff I really did, right here in this school. But God knows everything. Six months ago, I met God, met his son, Jesus, and now everything's different. I came clean with God; he forgave me and made me brand new. My record that you read of all the stuff I did, none of it happened after I met God. All that stuff is over, done with. The drugs, the drinking, the clothes I used to get in trouble for wearing, that's all gone. I'm clean, I'm new, and I'm trying to do the right things every day. God is helping me."

Christina raised her Bible in the air. "And this Bible is where I met God. I started reading it, and I met him! And whenever I get tempted, whenever I get pushed, whenever I think about going back to my old ways, that's when I just open this Bible and start reading! And God's words speak to me through his Holy Spirit! That's exactly what I was doing in study hall that day, reading this Bible, listening to God, and I won't let anybody, I don't care who it is, stop me from listening to God!

"So I'm begging you today," Christina continued, with tears streaming down her cheeks, "to let me stay in school and get my diploma. All that other bad stuff I did. And I'm sorry. Reading my Bible in study hall, I did that, too. But I'm not sorry for that. Reading my Bible is the only thing that keeps me from doing bad stuff. It just seems so wrong, so unfair, to punish me for doing the one right thing that keeps me from doing all the wrong things."

Christina didn't know what to do or say next, so she just stood there. The chairman asked "Does that conclude your testimony, Ms. Belle?" Christina nodded, wiping tears from her face. "Then you may be seated," stated the chairman sternly.

As Christina slid back into her chair, the chairman turned to the woman at the end of the table. "Counsel?" he asked.

The woman, in her droning voice, answered, "Mr. Chairman, members of the Appeals Council, the record now being closed, and no evidence having been presented to overcome the presumption that the tenth and final infraction was properly imposed, a motion to deny the appeal of Ms. Christina Belle and, accordingly, to immediately expel her from the River Regional School District, would be in order."

The chairman responded, "So moved." His motion was seconded and quickly passed 3-0 with no further discussion.

"You are hereby expelled, Ms. Belle," the chairman announced. "You must leave the premises immediately."

Christina didn't say a word. Still clinging to her Bible, she rose unsteadily and left Rivercrest High for the last time. Again she prayed silently, *Okay, God, I really don't get this...*

Counsel for Christians

In an era of increasing intolerance for Christian expression and a proliferation of "politically correct" speech codes, the use and even possession of Bibles in public school has become controversial. In the face of this growing hostility, many Christian parents and students have become unsure whether they can legally bring their Bibles to school, or use and study them there. There are several main legal issues concerning the Bible and Bible clubs in public school: the

First Amendment rights of Freedom of Religion and Freedom of Speech, along with Equal Access.

Freedom of religion is a two-part right. The government cannot act in a way that establishes religion, nor can it prohibit the free exercise of religion. Unfortunately many government officials—including teachers, principals, and school boards—are so afraid of offending other people that they trample on the Constitution! Furthermore, some of these officials are so threatened by lawsuits from organizations such as the Freedom From Religion Foundation, Americans United for Separation of Church and State, and the American Civil Liberties Union that they overreact in attempting to avoid any semblance of establishing religion. Often this means inadvertently prohibiting the free exercise of religion, effectively squelching a constitutional right in their overzealous effort to avoid violating a constitutional restriction.

Many parents and students might think that the only protection they have regarding issues of religious expression in public school is found in the Free Exercise Clause of the First Amendment. But religious speech is constitutionally protected under the Free Speech Clause, too! The Supreme Court ruled in *Capital Square Review and Advisory Board v. Pinette* that "government suppression of speech has so commonly been directed precisely at religious speech that a free-speech clause without religion would be Hamlet without the prince." So, students and their parents need to remember that they have a right to Free Speech regarding religion, too. But what exactly is *speech*? What about Bibles in school? Does free speech encompass only the spoken word? If so, then what about those physically unable to speak? Such flawed reasoning would mean that the Constitution does not protect individuals with speech disabilities!

It is imperative that an informed citizenry understands that the term "speech" applies to conduct, including nonverbal expression. In fact, the scope of the First Amendment is so broad that it is easier to describe what speech is *not* protected than to attempt to describe all speech that *is* protected. A few examples of unprotected speech include yelling "Fire!" in a crowded theater, some commercial speech, indecent speech, and pornography. Protected conduct and expression can be what we choose to read, believe, write, wear on our clothing, and so forth. Carrying and reading the Bible are activities that clearly fall within the category of speech covered by the First Amendment.

Furthermore, the Fourteenth Amendment applies the protection of the First Amendment to the states (many of which have enshrined their own vigorous state constitutional protections of religious speech as well). As such, the Constitution protects students from "the state itself and all its creatures—Board of Education not excepted..." as the Court eloquently stated in *West Virginia State Board of Education v. Barnette.*[15] The Court went on to say that specifically because public schools are educating for citizenship is "reason for scrupulous protection of constitutional freedoms of the individual, if we are not to strangle the free mind at its source and teach youth to discount important principles of our government as mere platitudes."

Regarding free speech at schools, the Supreme Court in its 1969 decision in *Tinker v. Des Moines Independent Community School District* said:

> First Amendment rights, applied in light of the special characteristics of the school environment, are available to teachers and students. It can hardly be argued that either students or teachers shed their constitutional rights to freedom of speech or expression at

---

15 West Virginia State Board of Education v. Barnette, 319 U.S. 624, 637 (1943).

the schoolhouse gate. This has been the unmistakable holding of this Court for almost 50 years.[16]

In that case, the Court determined that a mere fear of disruption was not a sufficient reason to restrict a student's right to free expression. The Court said that "undifferentiated fear or apprehension" is not enough to overcome that right. In order for schools to lawfully restrict high school students' speech, the speech has to substantially interfere with the school's operation. In the *Tinker* case, the Court also declared that public schools are not "enclaves of totalitarianism," nor do school officials enjoy absolute power or authority over their students.

It is a well-established principle that the First Amendment's Free Exercise Clause protects the right to believe and practice religion. In fact, this right is so established that Justice Kennedy began his opinion in a case called *Church of the Lukumi Babalu Aye* by stating, "The principle that government may not enact laws that suppress religious belief or practice is so well understood that few violations are recorded in our opinions."[17] The realm of heart, soul, and belief are so fundamental to our freedom that no government entity, including a public school, can determine legally what we feel, think, or believe. The Bible is not a banned book in school. In fact, the U.S. Department of Education, in 1998, distributed presidential guidelines to every school district in America. These guidelines specifically state that students have the right to carry a Bible and read it. If students have free time, they can choose to read the Bible just as they can choose to read any other book.

But what if that free time is in class? The same rules apply to the Bible as other reading materials. And it can hardly be

---

16 *Tinker v. Des Moines Independent Community School District*, 393 U.S. 503, 506 (1969).

17 Church of Lukumi Babalu Aye, Inc. V. City of Hialeah, 508 U.S. 520 (1993).

argued that reading is prohibited in schools, whether inside or outside the classroom. In fact, many schools have a study hall period in which students can do their homework, complete projects and class assignments, and study. Often students can use this time to read for pleasure, too. The mere fact that someone may be offended by a student reading the Bible is not reason enough to prohibit the foundational right to think and believe. Such exercise of religious freedom is clearly protected, once again as stated in *Tinker*, "...for the State in the person of school officials to justify prohibition of a particular expression of opinion, it must be able to show that its action was caused by something more than a mere desire to avoid the discomfort and unpleasantness that always accompany an unpopular viewpoint."[18] The "community inclusivity policy" referred to in the fictitious vignette at the beginning of this chapter would fall into that category of unlawful efforts to prohibit expressions of opinion based on mere desire to avoid "discomfort and unpleasantness;" constitutional freedom of religious expression would certainly outweigh such a school policy.

Bibles are allowed on school property because of freedom of speech and freedom of religion, but what about Bible clubs held on public high school campuses? A special federal law, the *Equal Access Act*, requires that any public high school receiving federal funds must provide "equal access" to all student groups, including Bible clubs if a few conditions are met. Besides the federal funding test, there must also be at least one student-led, noncurriculum-related club that meets on campus during noninstructional times for the Act to apply. An example of a noncurriculum-related club would be a chess club, model airplane club, political club, or a Bible

---

18 *Tinker v. Des Moines Independent Community School District*, 393 U.S. 503 (1969).

club; a Spanish club may be a curriculum related club. If any of these other noncurriculum related clubs exist, the school must allow access to Bible clubs in a like manner.

There are three legal requirements the Bible club must meet to comply with the *Equal Access Act* and not offend the Establishment Clause. First, it must be a voluntary club. There is no right under the Constitution or the *Equal Access Act* to force students to participate in a Bible club. Second, the club must be student led and student initiated. That means that a teacher or other public school official cannot lead or participate in the club. However, a school employee can be assigned for "custodial purposes." Furthermore, community or church leaders cannot regularly attend, control, or conduct the meetings. Third, the club must not disrupt the orderly conduct of the school.

But what if the school tries to circumvent the *Equal Access Act* by prohibiting all noncurricular clubs? The rights of religious students are still protected by the Constitution. The 1990 case *Board of Education of Westside Community School v. Mergens* determined that religious school clubs are allowed because of the difference between "government speech endorsing religion, which the Establishment Clause forbids, and private speech endorsing religion, which the Free Speech and Free Exercise Clauses protect."[19] The school must not engage in viewpoint discrimination.

Once a school allows access to school facilities by *any* student club, the school cannot deny that same access to a religious club because of its religious nature. Likewise, if a school allows student groups to use school equipment, the public address system, or school bulletin boards to advertise the club, then the school must allow a Bible club to do so as well. It would violate the First Amendment if a Bible

---

19 Board of Education of Westside Community Schools v. Mergens, 496 U.S. 226, 228 (1990).

club were prohibited simply because of its religious nature. Providing equal access does not endorse religion. Actually, allowing equal access to school facilities and benefits sends the correct message of neutrality toward religion. Remember, viewpoint-based prohibitions violate the Constitution.

There must be content-neutral reasons for imposing any restrictions on student speech, and they must be for the purpose of providing a safe school lacking in disruptions. The mere fear of offending someone does not permit a public high school to engage in viewpoint discrimination. Both the Constitution and the *Equal Access Act* protect high school Bible clubs.

Quick Counsel for Christians

★ Public school students have the constitutional right to freely exercise their religion.

★ This right is protected by the First Amendment, both by the Free Speech Clause and by the Free Exercise Clause.

★ Students do not lose their constitutional rights to free speech and expression at the schoolhouse door.

★ Speech is not only words; it includes conduct and expression, too.

★ Students have the right to read their Bibles in public schools just as they would any other book.

★ The Equal Access Act and the Constitution allow for student-led, student-initiated Bible clubs on public high school campuses.

★ Schools cannot censor student speech based on viewpoint or content. If a school policy restricts student speech, the policy must be content neutral, and there must be a compelling government interest such as ensuring a safe school environment.

Chapter 4

Excuse Me, You Want My Child to Write About What? Assignments vs. Conscience

J osh first heard about Mr. Andrews from his older friends at church youth group. "Just keep your mouth shut, and you'll be fine," they warned him. "As long as Andrews doesn't know you're a Christian, he'll leave you alone and you'll have an okay year in his world literature class."

"But if not?" Josh asked.

The guys answered cryptically, "Just remember, little Bro, we warned you."

I am almost sixteen, Josh thought, *maybe about the same age as Daniel, Shadrach, Meshach and Abednego when they were captured and then stood up for God in ancient Babylon. Certainly I'm old enough now to stand up for my faith like those courageous and heroic guys. It's time for me to be a man. I won't hide my true identity in Jesus from Mr. Andrews or anyone else.*

Most college-bound students took Mr. Andrew's class to fulfill their tenth-grade English requirement. The reading list, pretty standard, included some heavy works to digest, but it wasn't the books that made the class so challenging, it was Andrews.

A burly guy with an unusually loud voice, he looked disheveled yet carried himself with an air of pompous arrogance as though he held those around him in utter contempt. Although his intimidating stare was legendary around the high school, his stare wasn't what scared the students most. You see, Andrews knew how to make other people feel stupid, and especially how to embarrass and humiliate his students. And he wasn't the least bit shy about doing it. In fact, ruthlessly mocking and taunting certain students until they broke down in tears seemed to be one of the few classroom activities he truly enjoyed. It was the only thing that brought a smile to his face during class.

Although Andrews was capable of unleashing a relentless verbal assault on any student on any given day, obviously his favorite targets were students who revealed themselves to be followers of Jesus who held to traditional Christian morals and values. His very mission as a teacher seemed to be undermining and shattering the worldview of Christians who turned up in his classes.

Despite Josh's resolve to be a modern-day Daniel, during the first few weeks of school he stayed quiet in Andrews' class. In his heart, he intended to be a bold and courageous witness for his faith, yet he found himself timidly trying to avoid Andrews' potential wrath just like the other kids did. Then one day Andrews began toughly interrogating a girl he singled out who was a good friend of Josh's younger sister. As the girl began to stutter and stumble under the intense questioning, Josh's sense of chivalry finally overcame his desire for self-preservation, and he raised his hand to deflect Mr. Andrew's attention from the girl.

The subject under discussion was the "evolution and authorship" of the ancient law codes. Andrews forcefully taught that these foundational writings were "merely humanist expressions of the cultures in which they arose." He asserted that all laws, even ancient writings "attributed to Moses" such as the Ten Commandments, were "simply contrived by dominant human oppressors to impose their own self-serving paternalistic values and had nothing, whatsoever, to do with divine inspiration or any so-called god."

Knowing better, Josh valiantly tried to make his counter-point, explaining that there could be no true right and wrong apart from a God-given standard of morality. But Andrews, his skills honed by decades of tearing down the arguments of idealistic but inexperienced students, soon had Josh on the ropes. By the time the class bell rang, Mr. Andrews was wearing his trademark grin and Josh was shaken to the core, emotionally and spiritually.

Now that Andrews had identified Josh as a sincere Christian believer, during almost every class the same painful pattern occurred. Josh became the special target of a sophisticated and relentless verbal attack designed to completely destroy his faith and moral values—and, by extension, Andrews hoped to impact Josh's religiously inclined classmates as well.

When the time came for students to be given their first major writing assignments, Mr. Andrews had this special topic strategically picked out for Josh: "Why Tolerance and Respect for the Diversity of Humankind Require the Rejection of the Judeo-Christian Scriptures as a Source of Law and Morality." Unbeknownst to Josh, the list of mandatory reference materials Andrews provided for citation in the paper only included controversial works of prominent atheistic and radically anti-Christian authors.

Being berated and belittled by Andrews day after day took a heavy toll on Josh. One evening he thought, *I'm letting God down by being such a poor witness, such an inept defender of the faith. I'm not like heroic Daniel. I'm weak and, even worse, am losing what little faith I still have left. Now I have to write a big paper proving why the Bible is no good for anything.*

Josh's grades were starting to slip in all his classes; his attitude was slipping, too. He was too embarrassed to mention anything about Andrews to his parents, but after receiving negative progress reports from several of his teachers they finally forced the issue. Under gentle pressure, Josh told them the whole story, then showed them his world literature composition assignment.

Josh's parents were outraged and disturbed by the entire situation. "He wants you to write about what?" Josh's mother asked incredulously. Josh's father immediately recognized several of the notorious names on the required source list for the paper and quick online research confirmed that the rest of the materials were equally troubling. "Josh, this is an assignment intentionally designed by a grown man to destroy the faith of a fifteen-year-old kid!" he announced. "Your Mom and I are not going to stand by and let this happen!"

The three of them quickly formulated a plan. First, Josh went directly to Andrews the next morning and politely asked him to change the topic of the assignment. Mr. Andrews refused with a dismissive sneer.

Next, Josh's father wrote a cordial but firm note to Andrews demanding that the topic be changed. But when Josh delivered the note before class the following day, Andrews turned the parental request into a long tirade against "intellectually malnourished" Christians, eventually reading the letter out loud to the entire class in a derisive tone, much to Josh's horror. At the conclusion of the tirade, Andrews stated that the paper remained due as assigned.

The following day, Josh's father attempted to contact Andrews directly to discuss the situation by phone or set up a person-to-person meeting. But Andrews would not take the calls and did not return the several messages and emails from Josh's father requesting a call back. So, the next morning Josh's father contacted the school principal and requested a meeting with her, which she arranged for that afternoon. He specifically requested that Mr. Andrews be present at the meeting, if possible, and she indicated that she would invite him.

When Josh's father sat down in the principal's office, Andrews was not present. "Mr. Andrews has declined to join us," the principal explained, "He is relying on our academic freedom policy, asserting his right to control course content and student assignments within the parameters of state education guidelines, and he believes that discussing the situation with you would only be counterproductive."

Disappointed but not entirely surprised, Josh's father began describing a simple timeline of Mr. Andrews' conduct to the principal, emphasizing to her the pattern of deliberate attacks on Josh's Christian worldview, culminating with the paper assignment and Andrews' defiant reaction to his attempts to intervene on behalf of his son. The principal nodded but didn't seem particularly interested.

When Josh's father finished speaking, the principal spoke up. "Look," she said casually, "you aren't the first parent to complain about Mr. Andrews, and you won't be the last. He has been here for a long time, and he has developed his own teaching methods that work for him. He is a dependable and competent member of my faculty and has won many awards and honors over the years for his scholarship and longevity in the system. He knows his academic rights and that I will back him up one hundred percent."

Shifting in his chair, Josh's father listened in disappointment as the principal continued, her voice rising in intensity, "And you know what, I'm glad I back up Mr. Andrews. He is doing his job and doing it well, and sometimes his job is to undo some of that brainwashing that over-the-top, fundamentalist parents stuff into their kids' heads! And you can quote me on that because I've sat right here in this office when some of the very kids whose parents were in here complaining about Mr. Andrews come back in here later for one reason or another—they get in trouble or whatever. When they're sitting here in my office, they thank me! Do you hear that? They thank me for sticking by Mr. Andrews and standing up against their parents! Finally those kids get free from all that guilt, judgment, and moralism that parents like you push on them along with your Bible-believing nonsense!"

Josh's father was speechless as the principal concluded, "So let me give you one piece of advice. Tell Josh to get that paper done, on time, the way Mr. Andrews wants it."

Counsel for Christians

Whether in the form of government policies, rules, regulations or penalties, Christians increasingly find themselves forced to choose between obeying the law of the land and their own consciences. Rights of religious conscience have come under attack in almost every realm, from the imposition of immoral healthcare mandates to distorted legal initiatives that undermine the very structure of families. And public school students have certainly not been immune from this appalling trend. Rights of conscience are being legally eroded by government at the federal, state and even local levels. Yet, the rights of religious conscience have historically been protected by the Constitution.

The First Amendment to the U.S. Constitution states that "Congress shall make no law respecting an establishment of religion, or prohibiting the free exercise thereof; or abridging the freedom of speech, or of the press; or of the right of the people peaceably to assemble, and to petition the Government for a redress of grievances." But if the First Amendment specifically refers to *Congress*, the federal government, does it apply to state and local governments as well, where most public school policy is established and enforced?

This question has surfaced over and over again regarding whether the Bill of Rights—the first ten amendments to the U.S. Constitution—applies to the states or only to the federal government. The Tenth Amendment of the Bill of Rights reserves all powers not specifically granted to the federal government to the states. Power over the creation and operation of public education systems is not specifically granted to the federal government and therefore resides firmly with the states. State governments control policy and procedures regarding education, often through local school boards or other local political subdivisions.

The Fourteenth Amendment provides that no state (and by extension, no political subdivision of a state) can deprive any person of life, liberty, or property without due process of law. So what do life, liberty, and property include? The Supreme Court has ruled that liberty interests include those contained in the First Amendment. Thus the Due Process Clause of the Fourteenth Amendment guarantees the freedom of speech and free exercise of religion not just regarding the federal government but state governments, too. Because the issue of education is a matter left in the hands of state governments, due process requires that free speech and freedom of religion must be honored and protected in the educational system. Furthermore, parents' rights to determine the upbringing of their children are also applied via the Fourteenth Amendment.

As all parents know, one of the most important roles they fill in their children's lives is that of being educators. Parents and the entity of the family have the primary role of teaching—how to walk and talk and ride a bike; how to have good manners; how to understand and apply deeper issues regarding the foundations of the family's faith. Once children reach school age, parents still play an active role in their upbringing. The Supreme Court has frequently upheld the parental right to determine the upbringing of their children—including twice since the late 1990s. This principle is deeply rooted in the due process clause of the Fourteenth Amendment.

It has been described as a primary parental function and freedom to prepare children for adulthood and the obligations of living within society. The Supreme Court, in the 1977 case *Moore v. E. Cleveland,* stated, "Our decisions establish that the Constitution protects the sanctity of the family precisely because the institution of the family is deeply rooted in this Nation's history and tradition. It is through the family that we inculcate and pass down many of our most cherished values, moral and cultural."[20]

One of the most distressing issues that arises in the context of the education of children is the difficulty parents face when public school curricula conflicts with the students' or parents' religious or moral beliefs. This conflict manifests itself in a number of ways, such as when students are prohibited from expressing their religious beliefs in their homework, oral presentations, or artwork. Yet another area of conflict occurs when students are forced or compelled to complete particular assignments from specific points of view that are in conflict with their own beliefs. Notably, Supreme Court Justices Black and Douglas wrote in their concurring opinion in *West Virginia State Board of Education v. Barnette* that "words uttered under coercion are proof of loyalty to nothing but self-interest."[21]

Do parents and students have the right to opt out of particular courses, assignments, or teaching when they conflict with the parents' or children's beliefs and values? Or can the students be coerced out of fear of a failing grade to pursue their own "self-interest" to complete the offending assignments or courses? While parents clearly have the right to determine the upbringing of their children, courts have determined that right is not without legal limits. In fact, federal courts have not recognized a constitutional right to opt out of mandatory projects, assignments, or courses.

Thus, often parents are left with the difficult choice of either removing their children from public school or complying with the offensive assignments or courses. If parents

20 Moore v. City of East Cleveland, Ohio, 431 U.S. 494, 503 (1977).

21 West Virginia State Board of Education v. Barnette, 319 U.S. 624, 644 (1943).

choose to remove their children rather than comply, legitimate educational alternatives include private schools, charter schools, or home school. Certainly countless Christian parents choose these as viable options. But in the too frequent absence of strong school choice policies and initiatives, financial constraints may preclude parents from choosing the private-school option, and charter schools aren't always as readily available as they should be. And some parents do not feel equipped to home-educate their children. So what are parents to do when confronted with government imposition on their children's rights of conscience?

First of all, thanks to the 1978 Protection of Pupil Rights Act (PPRA), parents can exercise their rights to inspect their children's classroom materials. Parents can be involved in their children's public education by keeping abreast of what is in their children's curricula and also be involved in curricula review boards. These rights often do not extend to parents or other citizens seeking to inspect curricula of *all* children, but rather apply to individual parents regarding their *own* children. Generally speaking, parents have more extensively recognized parental rights regarding issues involving coercion than they do regarding issues of mere exposure. For example, the right of a parent to prevent the mere exposure of a student to a potentially objectionable topic such as evolutionary theory often is not protected. But when a child is forced or coerced into completing an assignment by endorsing a particular viewpoint regarding objectionable material, the courts have held that the Constitution provides more protection.

The *Board of Education v. Barnette* case involved a Jehovah's Witness who objected to the rule requiring all students and teachers to participate in the mandatory flag salute. Students who did not participate were sent home, then the respective students and their parents were subjected to truancy issues. In that case, Justice Jackson wrote, "Here, ... we are dealing with a compulsion of students to declare a belief.

They are not merely made acquainted with the flag salute so that they may be informed as to what it is or even what it means." He went on to write, "It requires the individual to communicate by word and sign his acceptance of the political ideas it thus bespeaks. It is also to be noted that the compulsory flag salute and pledge requires affirmation of a belief and attitude of mind."[22]

Anytime speech is compelled or coerced it must be strictly scrutinized, and the government must demonstrate a compelling state interest to lawfully impose such compulsion or coercion. Also, the government must demonstrate that there is no-less-restrictive alternative to the compulsion or coercion. In other words, parents have a stronger constitutional position to argue when compulsion or coercion are involved. However, the constitutionally protected parental rights apply to parents' own children, not necessarily children as a whole.

Second, parents can check with their state department of education and their local school board to see if there is an alternative to removal from the school. Because education is a state and local matter, many states choose to address the problem of morally or religiously objectionable assignments and courses via "opt-out" or "opt-in" provisions. Opt-out provisions allow parents to remove their children from courses and assignments they deem offensive or contrary to their belief systems. Opt-in provisions, on the other hand, require specific permission in order for students to participate in given topics, courses, or assignments.

Opt-in provisions cover things such as psychological testing and psychiatric care. The PPRA gives federal protection regarding psychological testing and psychiatric care in a program funded by the U.S. Department of Education (USDOE). If a child is subjected to these psychological tests

---

22 West Virginia State Board of Education v. Barnette, 319 U.S. 624, 633 (1943).

or psychiatric care, parents must specifically opt-in to have their child participate in a USDOE program.

The Supreme Court has not ruled on whether parents have opt-out rights, but other courts have. Even without a legally recognized constitutional right to opt-out, most states provide parents and students with at least some protection against offensive assignments and courses. Often this is accomplished by arranging for the removal of the child from a particular course or providing an alternative assignment in lieu of the offensive one. Some opt-out provisions are codified in state statutes; others exist in the form of local school board rules. Some provisions are very narrow and allow opt-out provisions only for topics regarding sex or health education issues. Others give broad discretion to parents, allowing opt-out rights concerning any topic including mere exposure to objectionable materials. Although some similarity exists between states' opt-out statutes, they vary greatly from state to state so it is always best to check with your state and local education departments to determine student and parental rights to opt-out of specific courses, assignments, or projects.

Quick Counsel for Christians

★ Parents have the constitutional right to control the upbringing of their children, including whether to send children to public, private, or home school.

★ Parents do not have a constitutional right to dictate the curricula of their children's public schools.

★ Parents do have a right to inspect their children's public school curricula.

★ Many states and local school boards have rules that allow parents to opt-out their children from offensive or objectionable assignments or courses.

★ The Supreme Court has not ruled on whether parents have a *right* to opt out, but the basis for parents to opt-out is found in the Constitution.

Chapter 5 ☆ Shush Children, No Talking About God! Witnessing at School

Miss Jennings loved her incredible kindergarten-ers. It was late spring of her rookie school year as a teacher, and she knew she had discovered her true calling. Each day the many hours of teaching flew by so quickly, and the kids were so much fun to be around. She never felt more alive than she felt in the classroom. Already she found herself dreading the rapidly approaching end of the semester and a long summer of missing her students.

The kids in her class came from all sorts of backgrounds and many different walks of life, comprising a truly challenging group for any teacher, especially a new one like Miss Jennings. Some children barely knew their basic colors when they started school in the fall; others came to school already reading and doing simple arithmetic. Miss Jennings did her best to serve all the students, working especially hard not only with those behind the learning curve but also investing herself in keeping more advanced learners intellectually and socially stimulated and engaged.

By the final weeks of the school year, many comfortable patterns and regularly scheduled activities had become part of the everyday routines of the kindergartners and their teacher. From nap times to snack times, from music times to story times, from quiet times to play times, everyone knew what to expect and when. Thanks to Miss Jennings' steady and gentle-but-firm leadership, everything kept falling nicely into place. The class had formed a healthy and happy bond, almost like an extended family having solid relationships and treasured traditions.

So a bit of confusion was certainly to be expected on the rainy Monday in late May when Miss Jennings reluctantly had to take a sick day and a substitute teacher unfamiliar with the usual, daily routine was called in to take over the class. But Miss Jennings had provided the substitute with a detailed plan for the day, and things were going well until late morning, when Miss Jennings' lesson plan called for "special time." Her notes explained that during special time she'd work intensively with smaller groups of students who needed focused remedial help or higher-level academic challenges while the other students enjoyed blocks of unstructured yet creative classroom playtime.

Special time was different each day of the week because Miss Jennings would work with different groups of kids depending on her assessment of their developmental needs. Classroom creative playtime for the rest of the kids had developed its own unique flow and rhythm for each day, too. Although some kids always liked to sit by themselves and draw or some formed small groups to play games, usually a larger group of kids liked to gather for pretend activities using clothes and props from Miss Jennings' well-stocked, dress-up boxes.

Some of the established favorites for pretending included "fancy restaurant" where the kids acted out being waiters, waitresses, and customers; "hospital" where the kids took on the roles of emergency doctors, nurses, and injured patients; "farmyard" where the kids became farmers and farm animals; and "rock band" where the kids transformed into energetic imaginary musicians. Another frequent favorite was "church" with a fiery pastor preaching to a small but enthusiastic, arm-waving, amen-shouting congregation.

The kids who played these pretending games always took to their characters with intensity. In playing "church," the kids would mimic every aspect of worship services they'd seen in churches or on television. Some even brought their Bibles to school to use during "church." They would sing, pray, and pass around a plate to collect an offering of old checkers Miss Jennings kept in the dress-up boxes as mock coins. And although Miss Jennings did not actively participate in any of the kids' pretending games, she always observed from the corner of her eye. As the daughter of a pastor, she always thought "church" was especially amusing and endearing.

But when the kids started playing "church" during special time on the Monday Miss Jennings was sick, the substitute teacher had quite a different reaction. At first, with her attention focused mainly on the small group of kids she was supposed to help improve their counting skills, she didn't really notice exactly what the other kids eagerly gathered around the dress-up boxes were doing. But before long, as "church" got rolling and the "pastor" started exhorting his enthusiastic "congregation" with shouts of "Jesus loves you!" it became inescapably obvious to her that something like a miniature Christian revival service was taking place among the children.

The substitute teacher was panicked by what she saw and heard. *I know this kind of thing is not allowed in school,* she thought. *I need to stop it right away! I'll never get a permanent teaching job if anyone finds out the kids were talking about Jesus in my classroom! I might even get taken off the substitute teacher list! I've got to act fast!*

Within seconds, the substitute teacher raced red-faced across the classroom, wildly waving her finger in the air and shouting angrily, "Shush, children, you can't talk about Jesus in here! Shush! Shush! Shush!"

The terrified and confused kids froze, but the substitute teacher wasn't finished. She was whirling and shouting over and over, "No, no, no! No God in school!" as she forcefully snatched up the Bibles and even the pretend offering plate from bewildered children's hands.

Finally regaining some composure, the substitute teacher took a deep breath and commanded, "Okay children, everyone gather around me and sit in a circle on the floor, now!"

The puzzled students meekly complied, and she launched into a long stern lecture, speaking slowly and clearly: "Now children, I don't know what Miss Jennings would say about this, but I'm sure she would be very disappointed in this sort of behavior. Everyone knows that we are not allowed to talk about God in school. It is against the law, and you could get into a lot of trouble if you break the law. Do you understand me?" The children nodded obediently.

"Okay," she continued, "so from now on you will never, never talk about God or Jesus or the Bible or anything like that in school. It is wrong to talk about God because it could offend somebody; it could hurt somebody's feelings. And we never want to hurt anyone's feelings, right class?" Again the children nodded.

Sensing a genuine teaching opportunity and still holding the rapt attention of the kids, the substitute teacher decided to make the most of it. "We must be tolerant. That means we must embrace–embracing is like hugging," she explained, continuing her slow, deliberate pace, making an exaggerated hugging motion and forcing a big smile onto her face, "We must embrace, we must like, we must love things other people believe in no matter what they are, so that means we should never, ever, talk about God or the Bible or Jesus. We must respect diversity, we must love things that make other people different from us, so that means we should never, ever, talk about God or the Bible or Jesus. Do you understand, children? Do you see? Do you see why it's so wrong to talk about God? You don't want to be bad, do you? You don't want to do things that are wrong, do you? Miss Jennings would be really sad if I had to tell her you were bad, wouldn't she? Wouldn't she?"

The kids all nodded. They didn't really understand why talking about God would hurt other people's feelings, or why talking about God meant they didn't love people who were different. And they didn't understand why Miss Jennings had never yelled at them for playing "church," but now they were getting into so much trouble for doing it. But they got the main point: talking about God is very bad.

Miss Jennings happily returned the next day to finish out the final weeks of her teaching. The substitute teacher didn't leave much of a report, just a few vague lines about accomplishing stated objectives, and Miss Jennings didn't even notice that the kids never played "church" again. There was too much going on, so many other games and activities, so much to teach and learn as the school year wound down to a close. Her days started to feel a little longer, and the kids seemed a little more draining and hard to handle. There were even a few fights and behavioral problems she hadn't had to deal with before. *Boy*, she thought, *these kids are really getting stir-crazy for summer. Maybe I won't miss them quite as much as I thought I would!*

Counsel for Christians

As we have discussed, students attending public elementary schools, middle schools, and high schools certainly have First Amendment rights! This includes the right to religious speech and any similar activities involving speech. But does this really mean that public school students can legally talk about God in school, or even share their faith with other students?

The Supreme Court decision in *Capital Square Review & Advisory Board v. Pinette*, clearly held that "private religious speech, far from being a First Amendment orphan, is as fully protected under the Free Speech Clause as secular private expression."[23] As with school prayer, public school students are legally free to engage in religious conversation in any places where other conversation is authorized. This means that the students' right to speak about a given topic during noninstructional times also extends to religious speech. And we all know how children like to try and persuade their friends toward their particular likes and dislikes. The same right applies to a student trying to persuade a fellow classmate to believe his or her way of thinking regarding matters of religion and faith.

In fact, matters of religion and faith are so integral to the fabric of American society that the Department of Justice's Civil Rights Division is charged with "combating religious discrimination and protecting religious freedom." This division even has a special section, the Educational Opportunities Section. The task of this special section is to enforce the part of the Civil Rights Act of 1964 that prohibits discrimination based on religion. This extends from elementary schools to high schools, and even to public colleges and universities. The United States attorney general, under Title IX of the Civil Rights Act, is authorized to file a lawsuit when a parent complains that his or her child is being treated unfairly or not being afforded the same protection under the law because of the child's religious views. The Civil Rights Division has been charged with this duty through the attorney general's delegation of authority. Furthermore, the attorney general can also "intervene" in any federal lawsuit that alleges discrimination because of race, color, religion, sex, or national origin, specifically when the case is of "general public importance." So, the government can be made part of a case that implicates discrimination based on, among other things, religion.

---

23 Capital Square Review & Advisory Board v. Pinette, 515 U.S. 753, 760 (1995).

In 2006 President Bush held a "Religious Freedom Day." He also issued a proclamation in which he said, "The right to religious freedom is a foundation of America....We reject religious discrimination in every form, and we continue our efforts to oppose prejudice and to counter any infringements on religious freedom." Under the leadership of Attorney General Alberto Gonzalez, a program was implemented to focus on what is known as the "First Freedom"—the freedom of religion. Not only is the freedom of religion first mentioned in the Bill of Rights, it is viewed as the foundation for all other freedoms. President Bush established a Special Counsel for Religious Discrimination to vigorously enforce civil rights threatened by religious discrimination, including the rights of individuals in the public educational system.

In early 2007, the Department of Justice released the "Report on Enforcement of Laws Protecting Religious Freedom." From 1995-2000, there was not a single investigation into religious discrimination in education. However, from 2001-2006 the Civil Rights Division's Educational Opportunities Section reviewed eighty-two cases and opened forty investigations involving religious discrimination. Fourteen of those investigations involved harassment by teachers or students; eight involved students' religious speech or expression. Some investigations involved settlements with school districts, and sometimes schools immediately corrected their wrongdoing. In other disputes, the Division filed amicus briefs. These "friend-of-the-court" briefs are filed by those interested in advocating on the subject matter of a particular case. The Division wanted to express the government's position on the particular issue of an ongoing court case.

One such case, *Westfield High School L.I.F.E. Club v. City of Westfield*, involved a group of high school students in Massachusetts who were suspended after handing out candy canes with a religious message attached. In that case, the Court agreed that the students' religious rights had been violated. In fact, Judge Frank H. Freedman said, "At the heart of the school's argument lies a widely held misconception of constitutional law that has infected our sometimes politically overcorrect society: The Establishment Clause does not apply to private action; it applies only to government action."[24]

In another case, *O.T. v. Frenchtown Elementary School District Board of Education,* the Division filed a friend-of-the-court brief in an elementary school dispute.[25] The New Jersey federal court agreed with the Division's position that a public elementary school student's rights were violated when she was forbidden to sing a religious song in a talent show because the song was viewed by school officials as "overtly religious" and "proselytizing." The school's music teacher had organized the talent show, and the teacher and a preview committee of two other teachers approved all performances. Students could not perform lewd songs or wear "revealing" costumes. Other prohibitions on the acts included "nothing...distracting, suggestive, depicting profanity, weapons, alcohol, drugs or illegal substances." If any teacher objected to a particular act, the school principal (who was also the superintendent) had the final say. The school refused the second grader's request to perform the song of her choice in the talent show, so her parents sued. Both of these examples indicate the Department of Justice Civil Rights Division's views on the importance of religious freedom, even in public schools.

In cases involving restrictions on student speech, two basic legal standards are found in two Supreme Court cases: *Hazelwood School District v. Kuhlmeier*[26] and *Tinker v.*

---

24 Westfield High School L.I.F.E. Club v. City of Westfield, 249 F.Supp.2d 98, (D. Mass., 2003).

25 O.T. ex rel. Turton v. Frenchtown Elementary, 465 F. Supp.2d 369 (D. N.J., 2006).

26 Hazelwood School District v. Kuhlmeier, 484 U.S. 260 (1988).

Des Moines School District.[27] Each of these cases addresses the issue of restrictions on student speech; one allows for restriction, the other does not. Although there is much confusion concerning which standard, *Hazelwood* or *Tinker*, applies in a given context, we know that constitutional free speech rights apply in the public school setting pursuant to the Supreme Court decision in *Perry Education Association v. Perry Local Educator's Association.*[28] The question of which standard applies to any particular situation hinges on whether the speech or expression in question is school speech or student speech.

A complex process known as "forum analysis" is used by the courts to determine what, if any, restrictions can be placed on speech purely based on content. Without getting too complicated, there are basically three types of forums where government can restrict speech based on content. It's easiest to understand if we think of it as a continuum with traditional public forum on the left, nonpublic forum on the right, and designated public forum somewhere in the middle.

Traditional public forums are places such as parks and streets where historically people can freely speak their mind. In order for the government to restrict the content of a person's speech in a traditional public forum, there must be a compelling government interest. This burden is rarely met because we hold the First Freedom in such high esteem, so the traditional public forum is afforded the *greatest amount* of First Amendment protection by the courts.

Nonpublic forums are usually not open to the public, nor are they set aside by the government as a place where speech can take place. Examples would be a military base or a jail where the government controls what happens there and the

---

27 Tinker v. Des Moines Independent Community School District, 393 U.S. 503 (1969).

28 Perry Education Association v. Perry Local Educators' Association, 460 U.S. 37 (1983).

public is not allowed free access. This forum is afforded the *least amount* of First Amendment protection by the courts.

The middle-of-the-road level of First Amendment protection would be afforded to the designated or limited public forum. The legal standard for this type of forum is the same strict scrutiny that applies to a traditional public forum. These are places where the public generally would not be permitted, but the government has opened it up for expressive activity. Examples would include a school classroom or city auditorium. The controlling government entity is not *required* to open up the forum, but once it is opened up restrictions to speech must be viewpoint-neutral.

In the case of a child's playtime activity inside a classroom during noninstructional time, the difficult question is whether a forum analysis or the *Hazelwood/Tinker* tests apply in a given situation. Regardless, the real issue is whether there was viewpoint discrimination. Whether a *Hazelwood* analysis (school speech), a *Tinker* analysis (student speech), or even a forum analysis (nonpublic forum or designated/limited public forum) applies, "viewpoint discrimination is...an egregious form of content discrimination. The government must abstain from regulating speech when the specific motivating ideology or the opinion or perspective of the speaker is the rationale for the restriction" according to the Supreme Court in *Rosenberger v. Rector and Visitors of University of Virginia.*

Sometimes the Supreme Court has applied differing standards depending on the age of the students involved. Under the above fictional scenario involving kindergartners, a court might find that the children were too young to fully understand the distinction between school speech and student speech. However, the Supreme Court, in *Good News Club v. Milford Central School,* explained that "whatever significance we may have assigned in the Establishment Clause context to the suggestion that elementary school children are more impressionable than adults...we have never extended our Establishment Clause jurisprudence to foreclose private religious conduct during non-school hours merely because it takes place on school premises where elementary school children may be present." [29]

Under circumstances described in that previous classroom scenario, the time was unstructured, the children were not required to participate in the pretend activities, and in fact some sat alone while others played games. Furthermore, the students chose a number of pretend activities for themselves. The teacher did not participate, either.

If your child faces such blatant discrimination, these types of facts must be analyzed in order to determine whether a government official's actions violate the constitutional rights of your child. School officials must be neutral regarding religious activity initiated by students, meaning there can be no discrimination or favoritism. Remember, a time cannot be set aside for religion, nor can students be prohibited from religious expression during periods set aside for free time. The Supreme Court, in *Rosenberger*, tells us that the Constitution mandates neutrality rather than hostility toward privately initiated religious expression. In the kindergarten scenario, the substitute teacher clearly expressed hostility toward the children's religious expression. If students are free to talk to one another, then they can talk with each other about matters of faith as long as the talk is student led and student initiated.

The Supreme Court made it very clear in *Sante Fe Independent School District v. Doe*[30] that not every message delivered on school property is government speech. Thus, the freedom of public school students to talk about God or witness

29 Good News Club v. Milford Central School, 533 U.S. 98 (2001).
30 Santa Fe Independent School District v. Doe, 530 U.S. 290 (2000).

to their faith at school remains intact. The bottom line? "The vigilant protection of constitutional freedoms is nowhere more vital than in the community of American Schools," according to the Supreme Court in *Shelton v. Tucker*.[31]

Quick Counsel for Christians

★ Public school students have a constitutional right to talk about God.

★ Public school students are free to talk about God anywhere other conversations are allowed.

★ Public school students are free to try to persuade others about religion and faith issues.

★ Public schools cannot discriminate against students based on religion.

★ Any restrictions of public school students' speech must be viewpoint neutral; if other speech is allowed, religious speech is also allowed!

31 Shelton v. Tucker Carr v. Young, 364 U.S. 479 (1960).

They've Crossed
the Line...

At Work

We Don't Tolerate Intolerance!
Diversity Training and Forced Indoctrination

Do Your Religious Stuff on Your Own Time!
Private Employers and Employees

Keep Your Church Out of Our State!
Government Employees

This Conversation Is Off Limits!
Witnessing at Work

Put That Cross Away!
Religious Expression in Your Office,
Locker, Truck...and Everywhere Else!

Chapter 6

We Don't Tolerate Intolerance! Diversity Training and Forced Indoctrination

Hank worked frantically, with one eye on the clock. There was so much to be done. Annual budget projections were due by the end of the week, pressing human-resources issues needed to be resolved, and a whole batch of time-sensitive, competitive bids had to be finalized and submitted. *The morning is going by so fast*, Hank thought, *and my afternoon is already shot. One of those mandatory, company-sponsored, management training seminars blocks my entire afternoon schedule.* As he often did when job pressures mounted, Hank took a moment to pray for God's help in using his time efficiently and effectively.

Hank accomplished everything he could squeeze in to keep his division humming, delegating the most urgent tasks remaining and reluctantly wrapping things up as noon arrived. Hurrying toward the training center on the top floor of the corporate headquarters complex, he tried to clear his head. *I hope I'll get something useful out of this session*, he thought as he bounded briskly up the stairwell. *Oh well, if nothing else at least I'll get a free lunch.*

As Hank entered the seminar room, he instantly recognized half a dozen of his peers, fellow divisional vice presidents mingling with a dozen or so less-familiar faces he assumed were up-and-coming junior vice presidents from outlying regions. Although today he would rather have remained in his office tackling challenging responsibilities, Hank loved people and was a natural at making them feel comfortable. Within moments, he was enthusiastically meeting and greeting, practicing his name-memorization skills and enjoying good-natured small talk and encouraging banter with colleagues.

Soon a woman Hank didn't know went to the podium and invited everyone to fill a plate for lunch from the catered buffet in the next room so the training session could begin. As everyone returned with food and sat down around large rectangular tables pushed together into a u-shaped arrangement, Hank realized he still had no idea what this seminar was about. He had been so busy during the previous weeks that he never bothered to open the entry his secretary had created for this event on his electronic calendar.

As the woman returned to the podium and introduced herself, Hank's eyes wandered to the slide projected on the screen behind her. A rainbow-colored logo with the words "No Boundaries" filled the screen, and at the bottom-right corner was a registered trademark symbol with the words "Loving Embrace LLC." *Hmmm*, Hank thought warily, *I guess it's time for our annual diversity talk from this year's trendy, new, outside consulting firm.*

The introductory presentation, just like so many others Hank had heard during his seven years with the company, was filled with the usual politically correct buzzwords about mutual respect and tolerance, and emphasized how important it is that these values be fully integrated into the corporate culture. Although some previous training sessions through the years seemed to include morally questionable ideas, Hank had never had a problem with living out most of the basic values they promoted. From the day he started as a shift worker in the warehouse and through all his promotions since, he had always treated coworkers with utmost respect and fairness. Now he continued to sincerely model those values to people he led and was convinced that those values had helped him become such a successful member of the corporate leadership team.

When the introductory talk ended and the woman began to explain the first participatory learning exercise, Hank was startled and disturbed by what he thought he heard. "What?" he said in a much louder voice than intended, drawing all eyes in the room to himself.

The seminar leader paused, staring at Hank with a pained expression on her face. Then she continued in a condescending tone, "As I was saying, as part of our unique, sensitivity-awareness enhancement methodology, my company has developed several cutting edge tools to help you successfully overcome your prejudices and cultural aversions. In a nutshell, by helping you face and confront your fears and artificially imposed boundaries, we will free you to truly embrace people different from yourself with unrestrained love and full affirmation.

"And so," she continued, looking crossly at Hank, "we will now proceed with our first, intensive sensitivity immersion module, a wonderful interactive exercise I like to call 'sensitivity through desensitization.' And, as I was explaining when I was so rudely interrupted, the module will involve simultaneous learning experiences specifically designed to stimulate tactile, visual, and analytical learning modes."

Hank listened carefully, trying to translate the overblown consulting jargon to make sure he had heard the woman correctly the first time. And, to his dismay, she repeated the part of her preview that nearly caused him to jump out of his seat. "Each of you has been randomly assigned a viewing partner, without regard to the archaic societal constraints of sex, sexual preference, or marital status," she continued. "We have commissioned the production of a twenty-minute video, artistically tasteful but intentionally graphic, in which our actors accurately portray various practices representative of the broadest spectrum of heterosexual, homosexual and polysexual behaviors. During the entire showing of the video, in order to facilitate the permanent breakdown of your own emotional, religious, intellectual, and physical boundaries, you are to hold hands with your randomly assigned partner and then, for ten minutes after the showing, discuss privately with your partner why each of the acts depicted in the film are to be affirmed and celebrated. Then, each of you will take several minutes to share with the entire group your personal affirmations and feelings experienced during this exercise. Now, here are the partner assignments...."

Hank's eyes scanned the room nervously, unsuccessfully searching for others who might appear to share his concerns. Although he was always a churchgoing and God-fearing man, he normally got along just fine in the corporate setting and didn't make too many waves. He willingly put up with a few policies, decisions, and training sessions he didn't fully agree with in exchange for knowing he had a great job he loved in a tough economy and was providing well for his family. But this afternoon's training exercise troubled him to the core. Everyone, including Hank, had heard cautionary tales around the office water coolers about the few employees who had objected to seminars in years past, none of whom kept their jobs for long.

I'm happily and faithfully married to my wife of nearly ten years, he pondered, *and now I am being required by my employer to sit and watch a porn flick in an uncomfortably intimate situation with another woman—maybe even a married woman—or maybe another man! I'll respect the values of other people that differ from my own, but I will not be forced into actively celebrating and experiencing those values.*

"No!" Hank shouted, springing from his seat, "No, I'm sorry, folks. I will not participate!"

The other vice presidents stared at Hank in shock. They all knew that these training seminars were at the very cornerstone of the company's cultural values. A rising young executive who refused to participate in the program was putting his entire career at risk. Yet Hank took his bold stand. After Hank walked out of the room amidst agitated whispers of astonishment, the presenter quickly brought the room back to order, stating calmly that Hank was an example of why training like this was so vital. "Men like Hank are the problem," she explained. "He's trapped in a prison of exactly the kind of small-minded and intolerant bigotry I'm here to liberate you and this company from. Now his hatred of other people and lifestyles different from his own is probably going to cost him his job, and I hope it does. We cannot allow people who think like Hank to poison the purity of the tolerance and diversity we all embrace."

Heads nodded in agreement as she continued, "We may never know what Hank feared or hated so much that he would refuse to allow his unhealthy and oppressive boundaries to be expanded for the good of this organization's employees and customers, but I'm glad he spoke up and left when he did. His presence and condemning attitude would likely have diminished the effectiveness of our boundary-stretching activities this afternoon. So, with that unfortunate episode behind us, let's continue. I'll stand in for Hank with his designated partner during our video exercise."

Counsel for Christians

So-called "diversity training" programs remain a standard feature of the twenty-first-century workplace landscape. Not surprisingly, however, the results of many scientifically conducted studies now cast serious doubt on the effectiveness of commonly accepted diversity training approaches.

Some data even suggest that these sorts of training exercises are counterproductive when it comes to achieving their outwardly stated goals of building an atmosphere of mutual respect and nondiscrimination among coworkers. Yet, despite this growing record of failure, many business entities and institutions persist in subjecting their employees to an ongoing parade of sometimes quite bizarre "diversity training" indoctrinations, all too frequently in the form of programs built on aggressive agendas openly hostile toward traditional religious faith and values held near and dear by many employees.

As it turns out, the real reason these disruptive and misguided sorts of training programs remain so prevalent in the workplace often has nothing to do with anyone's sincere belief in the ideals the programs claim to promote or any genuine enthusiasm about their methods. Rather, the programs are offered because management has made a cynically practical, economic decision to spend money on relatively cheap diversity training in order to help ward off or defend potential workplace discrimination lawsuits and keep overly aggressive government human-relations agencies at bay. In many other cases, diversity training is offered not because the executive team has willingly chosen to offer it, but because it has been imposed by a court or regulatory bureaucracy as part of a ruling or settlement in a lawsuit or administrative investigation. In any event and regardless of the reasons, employees now face a world in which the cottage industry of diversity training facilitation has grown into a permanently established and profitable business sector with operators of various levels of competency and moral judgment hawking their latest wares to the highest bidders.

Legal literature and court records in cases where employees have resisted or were themselves victimized by mandatory diversity training gone awry reveal some bizarre and morally misguided techniques apparently considered acceptable by those in the field. In the case of *Hartman v. Pena*[32] a government agency sued by an employee for sexual harassment and religious discrimination inflicted through its diversity training exercises agreed to settle the matter out of court. Among other indignities, the harassed employee had been required to run a gauntlet of coworkers of the opposite sex who were instructed to grope and touch his body, including his personal parts, while other coworkers humiliated and mocked him. The leaders of the training then made ongoing derogatory statements about the employee's religion to the group and refused to allow him to defend his beliefs. In other diversity training sessions required by that same government agency, even more egregious and disturbing methods were employed, including scenarios in which male and female colleagues were required to share a bed, coworkers were directed to use toilet facilities while tied together in pairs, and groups of employees were forced to shower together. For years thousands of employees endured such demeaning, immoral, and mandatory diversity training programs at that one agency alone.

What is an employee of faith to do when confronted at work with mandatory programs actively designed to undermine sincerely held religious beliefs? Is the only choice to run the gauntlet and suffer the spiritual, physical, and psychological consequences? Fortunately Title VII of the Civil Rights Act of 1964 prohibits religious discrimination in the workplace, even when that discrimination arises in the context of programs ostensibly designed to combat discrimination. Religious discrimination imposed in the name of tolerance, whether such discrimination is subtle or blatant, is not something an employee must tolerate!

Therefore, in order to comply with federal law, an employer should always provide employees with advanced

---

32 Hartman v. Pena, 914 F. Supp. 225 (N.D. Ill., 1995)

notice of planned diversity training sessions, specifying topics to be covered and methods to be used. If such notice isn't
offered, an employee is certainly entitled to request and
receive the curriculum in a timely manner from his or her
supervisor or the human resources department.

If, after reviewing the nature and content of the upcom-
ing training, an employee determines that such training
would violate his or her sincerely held religious beliefs, then
the employee should be permitted to skip objectionable
elements of the program. Obviously the employee needs
to clearly communicate the issue to the employer in order
to document the record and allow reasonable alternative
accommodations to be made. And, to gain necessary legal
protection under Title VII, the employee must be sure to
articulate the legally required objection that the training will
"violate my sincerely held religious beliefs." Also, the beliefs
themselves must be genuine. If this is done, the employee
will generally be legally protected from discharge, discipline,
or discriminatory treatment for failing to attend the diversity
training. If the employer refuses to respect the employee's
sincerely held religious beliefs, the employee has the legal
right to pursue remedies provided for under Title VII against
the employer, including the filing of a discrimination claim
with the U.S. Equal Employment Opportunity Commission
and/or any applicable state human relations agency.

Is it legally permissible for employees to speak out
against diversity training or similar workplace policies like
affirmative action? Yes. Can employers lawfully retaliate
against an employee who dares to challenge the merits of
such policies? No.

As Hans Bader aptly explained in his 2007 article for the
Competitive Enterprise Institute, "Diversity Training Backfires," as citizens we retain the right under the First Amendment and Title VII of the Civil Rights Act to criticize even
entirely legal programs. Our freedom of expression is not shut

down by virtue of our employment, and our employers do not have the right to exact retribution against us merely for being critical. As noted by Bader, in the case of *Sisco v. J.S. Alberici Construction Company, Inc.*[33], a federal court permitted employees' claims against an employer who retaliated against those employees for their criticism of the employer's affirmative action program. Likewise, in *Department of Corrections v. State Personnel Board*[34], a California appellate court prevented an employee from being fired just because he vociferously criticized a workplace affirmative action plan.

Not only do employees have the right to obtain notice of, opt out of, and even criticize diversity training that violates their sincerely held religious beliefs, it is interesting to note that sometimes diversity training literally backfires on the employer who requires it. For example, in another case described by Bader, when sensitivity training exercises encouraged managers to discuss their prejudices in the workplace, a federal court in *Stender v. Lucky Stores*[35], allowed those statements to be admitted as evidence of institutional discrimination and refused to dismiss an employee's lawsuit filed against the employer on those grounds. In *Fitzgerald v. Mountain States Tel. & Tel. Co.* (1995), a federal court warned that diversity training sessions reflect a "tyranny" of virtue, generating conflict and emotion!

Quick Counsel for Christians

★ You have the right to request and review diversity training curriculum from your employer in advance of the scheduled training.

---

33 Sisco v. J.S. Alberici Construction Company, Inc., 655 F.2d 146 (Ct. App. 8th Cir., 1981).

34 Department of Corrections v. State Personnel Board, 59 Cal. App. 4th, 131 (1997).

35 Stender v. Lucky Stores, Inc. 803 F. Supp. 259 (N.D. Cal. 1992).

★ You may notify your employer in advance that you wish to opt out of diversity training that violates your sincerely held religious beliefs.

★ Your employer cannot retaliate against you for opting out of diversity training that violates your sincerely held religious beliefs.

★ You are lawfully entitled to criticize diversity training programs.

Chapter 7 ✦ Do Your Religious Activities on Your Own Time! Private Employers and Employees

Maggie gulped down the last swallow of coffee as she reviewed her calendar. *It'll be a long day,* she thought, *but a good one.* She enjoyed working as a community outreach specialist for a growing regional bank, helping to spearhead corporate citizenship initiatives. Although her official job description contained many fancy buzzwords and jargon, the bottom line was that Maggie was supposed to be out and about every day, being the personal name and face (and eyes and ears) of the bank in its efforts to stay actively involved and highly visible in communities it served. She also made numerous stops at the bank's scattered branch offices and regularly participated in meetings at administrative headquarters.

Today, like most days, Maggie would drive from small town to small town, participating in a nonprofit board meeting, service club luncheon, ribbon cutting for a small business, and an evening charitable event. Her office was her car, and she typically left home by 6:30 a.m. and returned home after 9:00 p.m.

Although her lifestyle was intense, Maggie was energized by such interactions. She thrived on helping so many good people involved in various causes over such a wide area—everything from scout troops, pregnancy centers, soup kitchens, and after-school programs. Her great memory for

names and faces, combined with her genuine caring attitude, made her popular and appreciated. Plus, Maggie was
convinced that her position provided unique opportunities
to build honest friendships and gently share Christ's love
through words and actions. She believed her daily work had
the same kind of spiritual significance as being a missionary
in the field.

Maggie was grateful for her job, for the relationships she
had, even for the demanding pace. During this season of her
life, it was just what she needed. She graduated from college a few years earlier intending to marry her high school
sweetheart—a fellow graduate—the following summer, but
things hadn't gone according to plan. Her fiancé had gradu-
ally developed serious, alcohol-fueled anger issues during
their college years, and he got worse and worse after graduation. Finally he crossed the line one night and became abu-
sively violent with her. So, with much-needed support from
her parents and pastor, Maggie made the painful and difficult decision to end their relationship. She landed the bank
job soon after the break-up and happily and wholeheartedly
threw herself into her responsibilities as she worked through
a long, emotional healing process. *Sooner or later,* she'd think,
*the right new man might enter my life and my priorities may
change. But for now, I'll be content to keep working hard serving the bank and the local folks, doing what I love to do.*

Although her position was intended to produce mostly
hard-to-measure subjective results such as increased "good-
will" for the bank, objective statistics and customer surveys
consistently demonstrated Maggie's successful and positive
impact on the bank's operations. Many new customers—
individuals, businesses, organizations—cited their positive
relationships with Maggie as the top reason they opened new
accounts and did loan transactions with the bank. Employees at the branches and headquarters appreciated Maggie's

influence because they knew it created more opportunities for everyone as the bank grew and prospered.

I'd better get moving, Maggie thought. She placed her empty coffee cup in the sink, grabbed her purse and keys, and headed for the door. As she passed the full-length mirror in the entry hall, she smiled and winked at herself playfully, pleased that the fast pace of her job and occasional workouts at the health club helped to keep her fit and fashionable in the business outfits she wore. Just as she started the car, a text message from Shane Jackson, the bank's vice president of human resources, popped up on her phone: "Come directly to headquarters—need to see you ASAP."

Puzzled, Maggie guessed the short-notice, early meeting with HR likely had something to do with a potential new hire. Perhaps the vice president wanted her opinion on a job applicant he was about to interview, someone who had listed Maggie as a reference. This frequently occurred because she had built a vast network of friendly personal connections. *Well, I'll miss the chamber of commerce breakfast, but no doubt this pressing matter, whatever it is, will be resolved quickly and won't mess up the rest of today's packed calendar.*

Maggie smiled as she texted back quickly, "See you in thirty minutes—glad you start work so early, like me." The bank had hired Shane Jackson from a competitor about six months earlier. He caught Maggie's interest right away. He was not only a friendly, good-looking guy a few years older than she, he appeared to be single, too.

As she almost always did during her first trip of the day, Maggie used the driving time for daily prayers. By praying aloud, she could have a meaningful and reverential dialogue with God while keeping visually focused on the road. She prayed for loved ones and special friends, for her pastor and church family, for folks she knew were in need or distress, and for everyone she would encounter that day. She prayed specifically that in everything she did, in every interaction she had, she would be a good witness for Christ and draw people closer to him by her love, encouragement, and servant's heart. And, as always, she prayed for forgiveness and mercy for her sins and that she would have the grace to be merciful toward others in the same way God was merciful to her.

Not long after she finished praying, she reached headquarters and warmly greeted Shane in his office. On other occasions, Shane had impressed her as being fairly relaxed, someone she immediately felt comfortable around. Today, however, Shane seemed edgy and more formal, as if he had something to get off his chest. When Shane sat down behind his desk and began to slowly say, "Maggie, I don't exactly know how to tell you this," her heart raced. Her head swam with panicked thoughts. *I can't believe this. He is about to fire me. He is going to tell me I'm fired!*

Instead of the words, "You're fired," Shane was saying something Maggie had trouble comprehending at first. Seeing her perplexed expression, Shane tried a more direct approach. "Maggie, listen, I don't like this either, not any more than you do, but here's how it all went down. A few days ago, a new member of our bank's board of directors, the assistant dean of multicultural programs from the state university, started asking me a bunch of questions about you and your work. Apparently he'd heard our president bragging about you at the most recent board meeting—about all the business you've been bringing to the bank and especially how you are really effective at helping us start great banking relationships with many churches and Christian-based charities and their supporters. Apparently this guy has a problem with God or something because when I told him that you spend about half your average workday involved with churches and Christian ministry organizations in communities our bank serves, and that you are so great at it because you really speak their language and care about their success, he went ballistic on me. He started ranting and raving about civil rights violations, perceptions of institutional neutrality, and a long list of legal reasons why we shouldn't be paying you to serve and support any type of religious activities. Then he said, "Tell her that from now on she can do that religious stuff on her own time, not on the bank's time!"

Not knowing how to respond, Maggie sat silently as Shane continued, "I thought the guy was nuts, that he'd lost his marbles. Here he was telling me—basically ordering me—to make one of our most productive rising stars in the entire bank stop doing the things she does best just because he was offended or maybe he thought someone else might be offended if a bank employee did any outreach related to a church or religious organization. It made no sense, and I told him so. Well, that was a mistake. He stormed out of my office and right into the president's office. Last night the entire board had a special meeting all about you and the kind of work you do. They didn't invite me to say anything, but I got a late call at home from the president telling me to bring you in here first thing and order you to stop any community outreach you are doing for the bank involving any type of religious groups. From now on, you must focus only on secular activities.

"Look, Maggie, I told the president I didn't like this idea, that I didn't want to do this, that it wasn't good for business and wouldn't be good for your career. But he told me the board vote was unanimous, that their position was consistent with the law and had to be implemented, and that if I had a problem with enforcing their rules I should start packing up my things and he would start interviewing for a new vice president of human resources. So, Maggie, I hope you understand. No more Christian activities. Any questions?"

Counsel for Christians

There are many misconceived notions about the religious liberty rights private employers and employees working for them have in the workplace. In fact, often people seem to have the unrealistic expectation that they somehow have the legal right not to be offended and the legal obligation not to offend. (But, thankfully, this is still the United States of America and our Constitution provides no assurance against offense, nor does it restrict us from offending, even in the private workplace!)

But what about the "separation of church and state?" one might ask. Remember, the religion clauses of the First Amendment to the U.S. Constitution prohibit *government* establishment of religion but impose no such restrictions on private religious expression, including in the workplace. Although some people believe that religion has no place in public life in general, and in the workplace specifically, they are sorely mistaken. Private businesses and individual employees have every right to express their religious beliefs in the workplace.

This means that a business can certainly target its marketing efforts toward Christian organizations or churches just as a business could target their goods or services to any groups of people or types of businesses, provided there is no unlawful discrimination against others. A particular demographic, be it churches and religious organizations or bowling alleys and sports enthusiasts, is certainly an acceptable market for particular goods and services! Nothing legally prohibits a private organization from seeking to do business with Christian organizations or expressing Christian values. In fact, refusing to service a particular group of people because of their religion may even violate their civil rights. Think of it in the context of a business refusing to serve women or a particular race of people. That would be outrageous and illegal!

Often both state and federal law governs religious freedom in the workplace. The federal law covering most issues involving religious freedom in the workplace is called "Title VII." Specifically, it is Title VII of the Civil Rights Act of 1964. It applies to government employers, unions, and employment agencies as well as to private employers with at least fifteen employees at least twenty weeks per year. This same body of law governs discrimination based on race, color, sex, and national origin. Statistics show that religious discrimination complaints filed under Title VII have increased dramatically since 1997. In fact, according to the government's own data, the number of charges filed increased from 1,709 in 1997 to 4,151 in 2011, the last year for which such data is available.

Regarding religion, Title VII prohibits covered employers from:

★ Treating employees or job applicants differently based on their religious beliefs or practices.

★ Allowing or subjecting employees or job applicants to harassment based on their religious beliefs or practices.

★ Rejecting a request for accommodation by employees or job applicants based on their religious beliefs or practices, except if an accommodation will cause an undue hardship on the employer.

★ Retaliating against employees or job applicants based on actions taken to report or fight against religious discrimination.

There are two important exceptions to these requirements. First, religious organizations and religious educational institutions are exempt from the religious discrimination provisions. This means that a religious school or organization that is primarily religious in its purpose and character can give employment preference to those who share their same religion. Second, there is a "ministerial exception" that prohibits clergy from bringing claims under federal employment discrimination laws. The Supreme Court upheld the ministerial exception in a unanimous 2012 decision. The landmark First Amendment case, *Hosanna-Tabor Evangelical Lutheran Church and School v. Equal Employment Opportunity Commission*,[36] upheld religious groups' right to be free from government interference when it comes to selecting their leaders. Religious groups can determine who will be the mouthpiece for their religious messages, not the government!

Before we examine these issues from both the employee's and private employer's perspective, we must understand what is meant by "religion" under Title VII. Defined broadly, "religion" means all aspects of religious observation and practice, not just from traditional or well-known religions but those that are uncommon or even strange. This protection even includes beliefs or practices that are not widely held by the person's religious group. Interestingly, protection also extends to those who have no belief or practice if they are discriminated against because they *do not* believe. The law goes even further to protect those with moral or ethical beliefs as to what is right and wrong, even if they are not "religious" per se. Courts usually interpret beliefs as religious based on whether the beliefs concern core issues such as life, death, and purpose rather than on how strongly they are championed. Keep in mind, however, this does not mean simply that social, political, economic, or personal preferences are covered under the religious beliefs protection of Title VII.

Certainly this chapter cannot address employment law in every state, nor is the purpose of this book to provide

---

36 Hosanna-Tabor Evangelical Lutheran Church & School v. Equal Employment Opportunity Commission, (132 S. Ct. 694, 2012).

specific legal advice on a particular factual situation. However, plenty of attorneys can assist you with employment law in your particular state. Many states' laws require a strict adherence to a specific timeline in order to pursue a claim of religious employment discrimination. Often procedures must be followed in a particular order within a specific, often short, timespan. Some states even require that you file a state claim before you can file a federal claim under Title VII, or that you must file a state claim in addition to a federal claim.

The Equal Employment Opportunity Commission or EEOC, a federal bureaucratic agency, handles federal religious discrimination complaints. After a complaint is filed through the EEOC, an investigation and attempt to rectify the situation are attempted. If such a resolution is not successful, a letter to sue is issued so a legal remedy may be sought in federal court. Although specific, individual facts determine whether a worker has been subject to an unlawful employment practice, there are three basic components to a Title VII claim. First, the employee must have a sincerely held religious belief that is adversely affected by requirements of the job. Second, the employee must notify the employer of how that belief is adversely affected, and the employer must offer some sort of accommodation unless it creates an undue hardship. Third, the employee must have suffered discrimination or retaliation because of the job requirement or assignment.

Let's examine each of these components separately. First, sincerely held religious belief does not mean you need to be a "perfect" believer, nor does it mean that you have to accept every tenet of a particular faith. Furthermore, you can also have a sincerely held religious belief that is not necessarily required by your particular faith. In fact, a belief can be sincerely wrong...as long as it is sincere! A frequent example of religious accommodation requested occurs if an individual Christian believes that it is a sin to work on the Sabbath. Or perhaps her faith requires her to attend church on Sunday, but her employer wants her to work on Sundays. She must convey her religious belief and practice to the employer and explain how the job schedule conflicts with her sincerely held religious belief. Remember, the burden is on the employee to notify the employer. After all, how can an employer accommodate a religious belief if he or she knows nothing about it?

Religious beliefs and practices can include a number of things: attending religious services, wearing certain clothing or symbols, sharing faith. Some accommodations may only occur on special occasions, for example attending Good Friday church services or wearing ashes on the forehead on Ash Wednesday. It may be wearing a particular religious symbol, such as a cross necklace or pin.

Once the employer has been notified, the legal burden shifts from the employee to the employer. The employer is then responsible for making an attempt to accommodate the worker's religious belief or practice. Certainly the employee can suggest possible solutions, but the employer is not obligated to accept them. The caveat is that the employer is only required to accommodate the employee's sincerely held religious belief if it does not create an undue hardship to the employer. Unfortunately, courts have defined undue hardship in very narrow terms. Even so, that does not mean that mere inconvenience or a minor expense is an undue hardship. In fact, an employer must take seriously the duty to accommodate an employee's religious beliefs.

If the employer, after being notified, refuses to accommodate the sincerely held religious belief, the employee may file a charge with the EEOC and/or state or local agency. For the employer to prevail, he or she must prove that accommodating the employee will result in an undue hardship.

So what is a reasonable accommodation? Courts have held that any accommodation which imposes more than a *de minimis* (nominal or very minor) hardship on an employer is not required. However, an employer certainly has the option of going beyond the legal requirements. Realistically, a reasonable accommodation might require an employer to make an exception to a general practice or policy. For example, if all employees are required to work one Sunday per month, but a particular employee requests an accommodation, management may need to make an exception for that employee. But the employer would likely not be required to pay a substitute employee overtime to cover the Sunday shift. Courts have held that such a financial cost would qualify as an undue hardship. However, keep in mind that an employer can voluntarily expend whatever resources he or she chooses. Another alternative solution may be to allow a religious employee to voluntarily swap schedules with another employee in order to overcome the religious conflict. Such a practice goes a long way toward a happy and productive workforce. The employer must remember, however, that if a particular accommodation is made for one religious group, the employer will be expected to make a similar accommodation for another religious belief, even if such belief conflicts with his or her morals and beliefs.

Quick Counsel for Christians

★ Work does not have to be a "religion-free zone." Religious discrimination is not just wrong, it's illegal.

★ Employees' religious beliefs and practice are protected under state and federal laws.

★ Private employers with fifteen or more employees are generally covered under Title VII of the Civil Rights Act.

★ Employees have the right to express their sincerely held religious beliefs and practices, even in the workplace.

★ Employers are required to make reasonable accommodations to facilitate employees' religious beliefs and practices as long as such accommodations do not create an undue hardship for the employer.

★ Employees can file a complaint with the Equal Employment Opportunity Commission and state and local counterparts to resolve religious discrimination in the workplace.

Chapter 8 ☆ Keep Your Church out of Our State! Government Employees

D an Roberts came up the ladder the hard way. He attended a no-name, local law school at night while working full time to pay bills. He spent ten long, lean years in the public defender's office, pushed around by prosecutors, judges, and his own ungrateful clients. Then he became junior assistant district attorney. Now, as chief deputy district attorney, Dan knew he was finally doing what he was designed to do, the job he dreamed of when he started law school. He loved being on the side of the victim, making the world a safer place, taking dangerous criminals off the streets. He was good at this, and it showed. Yet he had no ambitions beyond that. The next rung on the ladder, district attorney, was more about politics than law, and he had no interest in the district attorney's corner office with all the trappings of political power. He was a lawyer called to do justice—humbly, fairly, mercifully when he could, and always with every ounce of skill, tenacity, and brains God gave him.

Certainly power changed hands after elections, and a newly elected district attorney could always fire and hire career prosecutors, but Dan wasn't worried. His reputation was solid, and he knew he was an important asset. After all, his success in the courtroom always made his boss look good in the public eye.

The latest election had been the same. Six months had passed since the new district attorney was sworn in, and Dan still felt secure in his job. The new district attorney wasn't the candidate Dan voted for, but she was the people's choice and he could live with that. But now she was doing something Dan wasn't sure he could live with.

Dan read her memo again, pondering the worn-out Bible on the corner of his desk. If nothing else, the memo was direct: "This is a public office, a vital arm of our government, and therefore, our employees must strive to avoid any conduct which might violate the constitutional separation of church and state. It has been brought to my attention that you prominently display a Christian Bible on your desk. The visible presence of this Bible may improperly create, in the minds of the public whom we serve, the appearance that the Office of District Attorney endorses or promotes certain religious beliefs. Further, the presence of this Bible is creating a hostile and threatening work environment for our employees, some of whom have already formally expressed their discomfort to me. Therefore, you are hereby directed to immediately remove the Bible from visible display."

I'm not an expert in religious liberties law, Dan thought, *but I'm not sure this is a correct interpretation of the Constitution.* Even so, Dan was prepared to comply with this order. She was in charge, and he served at her pleasure. And he only kept the Bible on his desk for convenience, not for show. It wouldn't be a big deal to put the Bible in an easily reached desk drawer. *I wonder, though,* worried Dan, *what happens when I pull the Bible out to read?* But where to keep his Bible was really the least of Dan's concerns.

During the early days, when he was still struggling to meet the overwhelming challenges of his work as a public defender and still grieving over the untimely death of his young wife, Hope, Dan became utterly demoralized by the never-ending stream of spiritually, physically, and emotionally broken clients he defended, so many of whom were obviously guilty as charged. He had been ready to quit, to give up on law and start a new life. But one night he prayed for God's help. And, he was sure, that night God led him straight to John 8, where Jesus skillfully and lovingly defends the woman caught in adultery even though he knows she is guilty. Dan believed this was an affirmation, a powerful encouragement from God to stay the course as a public defender for as long as it took. That night, he put the timing of his legal career in God's hands. And that same night, he got the inspiration to start a neighborhood legal clinic.

Hope Christian Legal Aid Clinic was a small operation, just a couple of rented rooms in an old church basement in the worst part of town. And Dan's vision for the clinic was simple. As he got to know the criminals he defended, he also got to know their families, friends, and neighbors. He became keenly aware of all the legal problems these folks were facing, usually without the benefit of a lawyer on their side. Landlords, employers, and even government officials were taking advantage of them. Through the clinic, Dan could show Christ's love for these vulnerable people by offering them real help, by encouraging them as God had encouraged him.

The clinic did everything free of charge. Dan quietly gathered modest financial support from a few sympathetic donors, covered the rest of the expenses himself, and relied on a sporadic trickle of volunteer help from other Christian lawyers and student interns from his old law school to supplement his tireless hours of community lawyering at the clinic. For Dan, who never remarried after Hope's death, the clinic and the people it served became his family.

The clinic had always provided legal help on civil matters only, never criminal law, to avoid conflicts with Dan's regular work in the criminal courts as a public defender. So, when God finally opened the door for Dan to switch to the prosecution side of the criminal law arena, Dan was able to carry on his joyful service of volunteer civil law work at the clinic without running into issues of ethical conflict. Now all that was in jeopardy.

With a heavy heart, Dan carefully reread the next paragraph of the district attorney's memo: "Furthermore, as a Deputy of this Office, your ongoing professional affiliation with the Hope Christian Legal Aid Clinic is creating an unacceptable public impression of government entanglement with, and support of, the overtly religious values and practices of that organization. For this reason, you are hereby directed to immediately suspend and permanently discontinue your legal work at Hope."

Dan set the memo aside, closed his eyes, and prayed silently at his desk. *God, I sacrificed so much for so long to prepare myself for this work as a prosecutor, and I knew you were with me, guiding my steps. How do you want me to respond to this memo? Do you want me to quit the clinic? Do you want me to quit the district attorney's office? Or, do you want me to fight this challenge, to stand up against this effort to purge you from the people's government? Lord, help me see the right thing to do, and fill me with the courage to do it. In Jesus' name. Amen.*

When Dan finished praying, he picked up his Bible and let it fall open in his hands. A business card he'd been using as a bookmark caught his eye. It was a lawyer's card sent by an old friend who'd gone to work in Washington, D.C. for a public-interest law firm. Dan had never paid much attention to the card before, but now the name of his friend's firm leaped from the page: Constitutional Center for the Preservation of American Religious Freedom. Dan smiled as he reached for the telephone.

Counsel for Christians

Where is that famous phrase "separation of church and state" found in the United States Constitution? Nowhere! It's not there! The phrase came from a personal letter Thomas Jefferson wrote on January 1, 1802, more than a decade *after* the Constitution was enacted!

Jefferson wrote to the Danbury Baptist Association in Connecticut to assure *them* that the U.S. Congress would not establish a government-preferred denomination or church! The letter was never about restricting the people in their private religious expression. But the old adage, "if you repeat a lie often enough, people will eventually believe it," certainly rings true in the context of popular debate on religious expression. Through the generations, Jefferson's comforting assurance of "separation of church and state" for the protection of minority religious groups from government oppression has been twisted and distorted by the anti-religious legal establishment to the point where many Americans now wrongly believe in a mythical "wall" barring religious people (and our ideas and expressions of faith) from government.

The abuse of Jefferson's words and the Constitution itself to oppress religion and promote a strictly secular government from which all Christian influence must be purged is the very opposite of what Jefferson intended! The First Amendment to the Constitution promises that "Congress shall make no law respecting an establishment of religion, or prohibiting the free exercise thereof." This clear protection of religious liberty in America was penned in response to the harsh restrictions and discrimination that religious minorities experienced under the system of government-established religion in England. The Constitution guarantees not only that the U.S. government won't sponsor an official (favorite) denomination or church, but also that it won't restrict people's right to freely exercise their religion—even in a government workplace!

Any employer, private or governmental, with at least fifteen employees is required to abide by the law under Title VII of the U.S. Code. This law prohibits firing or failing to hire a person based on a number of characteristics including religion. State governments are also required to follow Title VII, but most states have their own state agency charged with a duty to investigate claims of religious discrimination by state government employers. As such, many states have their own guidelines or laws similar to those of the federal government regarding rights of public employees in the workplace. Some state laws offer even more protection for employees than Title VII.

In general, *workers in government offices have greater protection of their First Amendment rights than do private employees.* This means that an employee—even a government employee—has the right to private expression of his or her sincerely held religious beliefs.

Many employers, including government employers, are so fearful of becoming targets of militantly secular legal groups such as the American Civil Liberties Union (ACLU) that they preemptively restrict the religious expression of their own employees just to reduce the risk of possible litigation. Meanwhile, because of the increasingly radical agendas of many opponents of Christianity, anti-Christian forces fueled by their long record of often-successful legal intimidation and bullying are becoming even bolder in their attempts to silence religious views. They may not hesitate to say things in the workplace calculated to chill free religious expression, comments such as, "You should keep your religion private" or "I am offended by your religion." But remember, the Constitution doesn't guarantee anyone's right not to be offended; what it does guarantee is an employee's right to express religious views, even if somebody is offended by them!

In Luke 12:8-9, Jesus Christ explicitly says that "whoever acknowledges me before men, the Son of Man will also acknowledge him before the angels of God. But he who disowns me before men will be disowned before the angels of

God." As disciples of Jesus, we are called to be true to our faith wherever we are, even in the government workplace.

The Constitution prohibits the suppression of speech based on content or viewpoint. There is no such thing as "freedom *from* religion" in America. A personal workspace in a government agency, such as an office or cubicle or vehicle, can be used for personal religious expression as long as it doesn't interfere with government function. If other government employees are allowed to keep personal items on their desks, then a Christian can keep a Bible on his or her desk, too.

A government employee also has the liberty to read the Bible during breaks and lunch, even on government property (but only, of course, on personal time). A Bible on an employee's desk might raise legal issues if it is in a public space where the public could legitimately confuse personal religious belief with the government establishing a religion, but in reality this is hardly ever the case.

Just because another employee is "offended" by a Bible does not mean the Bible's owner is required to remove it. That would be unconstitutional viewpoint discrimination. The same holds true for all types of employee speech. If an employer allows "small talk" during work hours, then for the employer to permit "any small talk except religious talk" would likely be considered unlawful viewpoint discrimination. However, the government employer does have a right to regulate or limit an employee's private speech when the efficiency of the government operation is affected. (During work hours, for example, the employee is paid to do the work of the government, not pursue a personal agenda, religious or otherwise.)

In general, the government employer can't restrict an employee's speech outside the workplace, either. The only legally acceptable restrictions on off-duty religious activities are neutral restrictions that apply to all off-duty conduct.

If there is no prohibition on other types of volunteer work, for example, a supervisor can't prohibit an employee's off-duty volunteer work because of its religious nature. One possible exception would be if the speech somehow affected the employee's ability to do his or her job. Judges, for example, are public employees who can be restricted as to what they say outside of the workplace, but they are certainly not precluded from serving in their churches just because they are judges. It would be blatant discrimination if we told all of the judges in America that they can't go to church because they are judges!

Quick Counsel for Christians

★ You can privately express your sincerely held religious belief, even at your government job.

★ You can freely speak and practice your religion outside of your government job as long as it doesn't affect your work.

★ You can keep things in your personal workspace at your government job, even religious items like your Bible, if other employees can keep things in their personal workspace.

★ A government employer can't refuse to hire you based on your religion.

★ A government employer can't limit your off-duty religious activities more than the employer limits any other employee's off-duty activities.

★ A government employer can't fire you based on your religion.

Chapter 9 ✶

This Conversation Is Off-Limits! Witnessing at Work

At sixty-one, Rick was the oldest guy in the warehouse by more than a decade. Most of the crew he started with had long since been promoted into management or moved on to other careers, but Rick was satisfied to stay where he was. The money and benefits were solid, and his seniority gave him job security during tough economic times when layoffs swept the company. Most important of all, it was the kind of job he could leave behind at the end of his eight-hour shift each day without dragging home additional pressures or responsibilities. Rick needed that kind of freedom in order to pursue his true mission in life: serving as chief Bible teacher, counselor, and evangelist for the one-man prison ministry he'd been conducting faithfully for more than twenty years.

Almost every weeknight after his shift at the warehouse, Rick would spend several hours leading a full schedule of long-running Bible studies and Christian discipleship groups at one of the county jails or state penitentiaries within a one- to two-hour drive of his modest home. On weekends, he would hit the road for other correctional facilities anywhere within a day's drive where he'd stay in cheap motels on Saturday nights and both preach and lead Sunday evangelistic services at prison chapels before returning home late on Sunday evenings. After so many years of diligent ministry, all the prison wardens and chaplains knew Rick and trusted him implicitly, convinced of his effectiveness by the steady fruit of inmates experiencing transformed attitudes and lives as a result of his anointed ministry.

As Rick often explained, he hadn't started his prison ministry by choice. Instead, when he hit his personal low point in his late thirties—drinking more and more, dabbling in drugs, losing his marriage after a string of affairs and selfish behavior, he suddenly and unexpectedly encountered God. He couldn't really explain it, but one night he opened a dusty Bible he found in his shabby bachelor apartment. Not only did he end up receiving Jesus as Lord and Savior and being miraculously delivered from his destructive habits and attitudes, he was powerfully convicted that he was supposed to start bringing the Gospel of Jesus Christ to prisoners. This conviction was so strong and overwhelming he felt compelled to obey. He had learned a lot since his conversion about theology, Christian counseling, preaching, prayer, patience, and forgiveness, and the conviction to minister to inmates remained just as clear and inescapable. He felt richly blessed to be doing God's work in serving "the least of these."

Years of working with inmates had taught Rick more than he ever would have dreamed about human nature and personalities. Entering into the rough and ugly world of prison life, Rick quickly learned—sometimes the hard way—how to spot phonies and manipulators, and how to rapidly discern evolving group dynamics.

Accustomed to the heightened level of situational awareness he developed in order to survive and minister effectively in prison culture, seeing through usual workplace drama and petty politics of his warehouse job became easy for Rick. At times he used his skills of subtle discernment to sniff out criminal conduct, such as when he uncovered and reported a ring of coworkers stealing warehoused goods. Mostly he tried to use his fluency in "reading people" to spot coworkers in personal crisis, folks he might be able to help rescue from potentially disastrous consequences of their own poor choices.

Rick was never pushy or judgmental in the way he approached coworkers, but he wasn't shy either when it came to discussing mistakes he had made, the permanent damage and pain he had caused himself and others, and how Christ had forgiven and delivered him. Just like with the inmates to whom he ministered, he found that building genuine relationships with coworkers and then sharing his experiences in a gritty and honest way, without sugar coating, was most effective in guiding them to Christ and receiving healing power. During the years, he led several coworkers into saving relationships with Christ and successfully encouraged dozens of others to turn away from their destructive paths, usually doing most of his counseling and witnessing over lunches or coffee in the company break room.

One day Rick began keeping a gently watchful eye on Bethany, a wife and mother who had recently started working in the warehouse on day shift while her husband, a local police officer, worked an overnight beat. Bethany had been married about ten years. With two small children at home, the staggered work schedules meant that either she or her husband could almost always be with their kids. But, as Rick knew too well, it also opened the door to potential trouble.

Within just a few months of Bethany's hire, Rick started seeing unmistakable signs that trouble had arrived. Bethany began spending most of her breaks in the maintenance supervisor's office, often with the door closed. Then she and the supervisor took a simultaneous half-day of personal leave and, when Rick left work at the end of their regular shift Bethany's car was still parked in her usual spot in the employee lot. Worried, Rick prayerfully resolved to do his best to help Bethany.

When Rick saw Bethany heading for the break room around lunchtime later that week, he struck up a friendly conversation with her. They had chatted briefly a few times before, and when Rick asked if it would be okay to talk during lunch Bethany cheerfully agreed. Their light discussion at a small table on the perimeter of the room ebbed and flowed comfortably. When the time seemed right, Rick decided to tell aspects of his life story, highlighting mistakes he made and their damaging consequences—especially those related to his failed marriage. Bethany listened, growing quieter and shifting self-consciously in her seat.

Finally Rick bluntly shared his concern. "Bethany, I don't want to see you to go down the same destructive path I did. I don't want to see you destroy your marriage like I destroyed mine. I didn't turn to Jesus for help until it was too late, but you can turn to him now, and...," Rick sputtered to a pause as Bethany jumped to her feet, her face reddening with anger.

"Look, you self-righteous busybody, trying to stick your nose in everybody else's business," she shouted. "Who made you my judge? I'm thirty years old; I can make my own decisions. I sure don't need you busting on me trying to label me as some slut, putting a big guilt trip on me, and pushing your Jesus nonsense down my throat! This is a free country! As old as you are, you should know better than talking to people about that phony-baloney hypocritical garbage, especially at work of all places! This whole conversation is off-limits, and you know it! If you don't back off, I'm going to report you and get you fired! Do you understand? Back off!" Then Bethany whirled and stormed out of the room.

Rick sat alone, feeling the stares of the half-dozen of coworkers whose lunch breaks were interrupted by Bethany's loud tirade. The man nearest to Rick was Justin, a fork-lift driver. Justin glanced around the now-quiet room and said, "Rick, don't let her scare you. Keep doing what you do, Brother. If you hadn't called me out four years ago when I was getting into all that dope smoking, I'd probably be living in a homeless shelter by now, spaced out and without my wife and my kids. You saved my future, man, you really did, and I thank you for it!"

Colleen, an order processor, then spoke up. "Rick, I'm not going into the details, but you know them. Maybe I never really thanked you before because I was too embarrassed, but you were the only one with the guts to talk to me, the only one who cared enough to say something to my face instead of gossiping behind my back." As tears filled her eyes, she finished, "Well, I thank you too, and my husband thanks you, and my kids thank you."

Then Jimmy thanked Rick for warning him not to fall in with the guys who ended up in jail for stealing merchandise. Lisa, thanked Rick for encouraging her to turn back to God. Sari thanked Rick for being the first person to tell her about Jesus. And then, all of them surrounded a tearful yet smiling Rick and gave him affectionate slaps on the back, hugs, and high fives.

Counsel for Christians

Today many people would say that religion has no place in public life, particularly in the workplace. But our founding fathers thought otherwise, hence the reason why religious expression and freedom from government entanglement in religion are included in the Bill of Rights. Many followers of Jesus would argue, "The very nature of our Christian faith is such that we want to share what Christ has done for us with other people so that they also find salvation in Jesus."

Certainly witnessing in the workplace is particularly challenging. On one hand, if employees complain to management about an employee or supervisor's proselytizing, management is required to address the complaints or face potential legal consequences. But on the other hand, if an

employer requires a religious employee to cease witnessing, the employer could also be liable for failing to accommodate that employee's right to exercise religious faith! So,
both employers and employees need to understand the legal
parameters regarding religious freedom—even witnessing—
in the public or private workplace.

Proselytizing or witnessing at work can sometimes be mis-
construed or mischaracterized as religious harassment. An
employer must balance the duty to take prompt action against
claims of harassment with the duty to accommodate employees' religious exercise. And, likewise, the freedom a follower
of Jesus has to share his or her faith must be exercised in a
manner that does not rise to the level of harassment. In fact,
religious harassment is legally assessed using the same criterion as other forms of harassment, like sexual harassment or
harassment based on race, color, or national origin.

Religious harassment is prohibited under both state and
federal law. States may offer more protection against religious discrimination, but at a minimum Title VII of the Civil
Rights Act of 1962 prohibits religious harassment. Religious
harassment violates the law in two instances. The first one
is known as *quid pro quo* and occurs when an employee is
"required or coerced to abandon, alter, or adopt a religious
practice as a condition of employment" according to the
Equal Employment Opportunity Commission, the government entity that handles employment-related discrimination. *Quid pro quo* harassment can also give rise to claims of
disparate treatment or refusal to accommodate a sincerely
held religious belief. The second type of religious harassment occurs when a person is subjected to unwanted religious conduct or conversation that is "so severe or pervasive"
that the individual claiming harassment feels as though the
workplace has become hostile or abusive. If a work environment is deemed hostile or abusive, the employer can be held
legally liable. If a supervisor is the source of this conduct and

the employer fails to address it, the company will potentially be held legally liable for the supervisor's conduct.

What does religious coercion look like? It can take different forms. For example, if a Christian supervisor attempts to persuade an employee to return to her Christian faith, that would not likely be considered religious coercion. But if the supervisor tells the employee that she needs to return to her faith in order to be promoted within the company, that would likely be deemed coercion. Likewise, if an employer tries to persuade an employee to abandon his Wiccan faith and allocates choice assignments only to those employees who share the employer's religion, that would likely amount to religious harassment because the employer attempted to persuade the employee to abandon his or her faith.

Some forms of religious coercion are more subtle. For example, if an employee has a sincerely held religious belief requiring observance of a Friday evening Sabbath, she can request an accommodation of her work schedule to allow her to depart early on Fridays to observe this religious mandate. The employer would be obeying the law by granting this accommodation. However, the employer could still be liable for religious harassment if he or she only schedules meetings, trainings, and client appointments on Friday afternoons when the religious employee is off. Notice, in this example the supervisor does not specifically mention religion when scheduling the meetings and trainings, yet it is still because of religion that he or she is acting. This is also religious harassment.

Witnessing in the workplace must be addressed from both employee and employer perspectives. An employee may be subjected to a hostile work environment if he has been harassed, based on his religious views, with unwelcome comments to such an extent that it renders the workplace intimidating, hostile, or offensive. The applicable legal standard is that the harassment must be "severe or pervasive." A work environment may be deemed hostile to the point of severity if the targeted employee is threatened based on his or her religious views, even if it only happens once. An example of a one-time occurrence that may rise to the level of severe would be one in which the employee's life, safety, or family is physically threatened.

Business owners who seek to honor God in their businesses also need to be cautious of religious discrimination, which may take the form of mission statements or written policies. Often an overtly Christian employer attracts like-minded employees. That is perfectly acceptable as long as employees and job applicants outside the faith, or those who wander from their faith after joining the company, do not feel pressured or coerced into adopting the faith of the majority. One way for Christian employers to avoid running afoul of the law is to conduct training for all managerial and supervisory personnel. Such training should include education in religious discrimination, written policies on discussing matters of personal faith with subordinates, and written procedures for handling harassment complaints. Furthermore, all employees should know what conduct is acceptable and understand anti-harassment policy and procedures for the respective company. All employees, regardless of faith, should know that their concerns will be taken seriously, investigated fully, and handled appropriately. Mission statements should be worded carefully so that adoption of the employer's faith is not implied as a condition of employment or advancement.

To rise to the level of religious harassment, conduct must first be unwelcome, but it cannot merely be assumed that all witnessing will be unwelcome. An employer's blanket prohibition on witnessing in the workplace would be just as legally problematic as an employer not properly addressing unwelcome conduct. How many times have you, or someone you know, been subjected to a person using Jesus' name as an expletive? This is offensive, but all the surrounding circumstances must be assessed to determine if something is legally considered to be unwelcome conduct. For example, the conduct of a co-worker or supervisor who repeatedly ridicules an employee's faith or religious preferences may be obviously unwelcome based on the employee's reaction to the ridicule.

Just because a conversation is religious, however, doesn't mean that it is unwelcome. For example, if two employees were discussing their faith in the lunchroom during a coffee break, it would not be considered unwelcome. Because they were engaged in a consensual dialogue, even if another coworker is offended or upset by their conversation it probably would not be considered unwelcome. Just because a religious conversation is overheard by others does not make it legally unwelcome.

The issue of *welcome* versus *unwelcome* is critically important when it comes to witnessing. The key thing to remember is if a person being witnessed to in the workplace asks the witnessing person to stop, that request must be respected. Certainly the witnessing person can pray for that person, treat him or her with respect, and continue to reach out in Christian love. If the witnessing continues after such a request, the employer can be held responsible. If an employee complains to his or her employer about the witnessing, or the employer knows or should have known that the conduct is unwelcome, the employer must address the situation or face legal consequences.

Not all religious comments or conversations in the workplace rise to the level of being unlawful. Remember, the conduct must be severe or pervasive in the eyes of a reasonable person. Some guidelines to look out for include whether the conduct is derogatory, offensive, frequent, threatening, or humiliating. Insensitive comments usually do not rise to the level of creating a hostile work environment. One way to assess whether a reasonable person would find a comment severe or pervasive would be to determine if it would alter the conditions of employment to the point of being discriminatory. Keep in mind that circumstances can rise to the level of being unlawful without affecting an employee's production. The Supreme Court specifically addressed the fact that a dedicated employee should not be penalized if she maintains the level of production in spite of the religious discrimination. If comments are not directed at the complaining employee, they usually will not create a hostile work environment as long as the comments are not abusive in nature.

Quick Counsel for Christians

★ Employees and employers have the right to witness in the workplace as long as they stop if asked by the person they are sharing with or by a supervisor.

★ Religious discrimination occurs if an employer or supervisor explicitly ties a job benefit or avoidance of sanction to the employee's abandonment, alteration, or adoption of a particular religious belief or practice.

★ For witnessing to be considered religious harassment, it must be:

    ☆   Unwelcome

    ☆   Severe or pervasive

    ☆   Impactful on coworkers or work performance

★ Employees and employers can pray or read Scripture at company meetings and events as long as objecting employees are not required to participate.

★ Religious activity cannot be a term or condition of employment, nor can an employee be penalized for refusing to participate.

★ Customer preference is not a legitimate reason to exclude religious activity from the workplace.

Chapter 10

Put That Cross Away! Religious Expression in Your Office, Locker, Truck...

Jake eased his red pickup truck into a parking spot outside the plant, grabbed his lunch cooler and Bible, and climbed out into the early dawn light. His steel-toed work boots crunched noisily in the gravel as his eyes shot an appreciative glance at his new, customized "1GOD4ME" license plate reflecting the first glints of sunrise. Entering the building, empty except for the night-time cleaning crew finishing their shift, Jake popped open his locker, then paused to contemplate a few of the Christian-themed stickers, inspirational quotes, and Bible verses covering the door.

Checking the time, Jake stowed his lunch, grabbed a stack of study guides and a few CDs from the top shelf, and closed the locker. He headed down the corridor and into the battered company conference room, flipping on the light and starting coffee in the old percolator. As the coffee brewed, Jake put one of his favorite worship-music CDs into the dusty boom box, pulled a rickety metal folding chair up to the well-worn table, and sat down for a last-minute review of the Scripture passage he read last night in preparation for the Bible study he would soon lead for coworkers.

As the first people filtered into the room, Jake greeted each enthusiastically, handing out study guides and asking about their families or various personal matters with which they were dealing. Conversations were relaxed; this was a safe and comfortable place for people to be honest and caring with each other. Jake sometimes enjoyed the few minutes before Bible study as much as the study itself because his coworkers reminded him of how much they had come to know and trust him, each other, and God during the three years since he came up with the crazy idea of running a weekly Bible study at an hour when most employees would normally be getting ready for another long day of work.

Although Jake struggled in the beginning to recruit the first few participants, that turned out to be easy once positive word of mouth about the group started to spread throughout the plant's hundreds of employees. The real challenge Jake faced was getting the boss, who was the owner and chief executive officer of the plant, to authorize the idea of a Bible study in the first place. A hardhearted penny pincher, the boss had a well-known disdain for organized religion in general and Christianity in particular. To get an affirmative response, Jake had to convince him that bringing employees together in a voluntary Bible study session would be good for morale and productivity, in other words good for the bottom line. Finally the boss agreed, reluctantly, to let Jake proceed on a trial basis. "But," the boss warned, "if people are late to work because of this study or if I hear any complaints from other workers about 'you Jesus people bothering them,' it'll be over." So far, there hadn't been any problems.

Soon it was time to begin the morning's study, and Jake surveyed the room. Nearly twenty-five people—laborers and sales executives, engineers and machine operators, managers and mechanics—were laughing, chatting, and sipping coffee. *It's still hard to believe so many people are willing to come in here so early*, Jake thought as he switched off the CD player. Just as he was about to call everyone together around the tables for the opening prayer, he noticed something was missing. "Hang on everyone," Jake said with a slightly embarrassed smile, "I almost forgot the cross!"

As Jake raced to his locker to retrieve the foot-high metal cross he always placed at the center of the largest table during the Bible study, he pondered the unintentionally self-convicting power of the words he had just uttered. *I almost forgot the cross! How true and how frightening! How many times during each day does that happen to me! How often do I forget about the cross, about what Jesus did for me!*

By the time Jake returned and placed the cross in its usual place of honor, he was pretty sure he wouldn't need the study guides to lead the lesson. Today's discussion would be about how easy it is for believers to forget the cross, to live as if they never even heard of Jesus. And Jake would get the discussion rolling by confessing his failures of faith, even with all the reminders he always kept around.

Jake prayed, then gave an opening testimonial. "Folks, many of us have gotten to know each other pretty well through this Bible study, and I think we've all grown a lot closer to God through our studies and discussions. As far as I know, there's not one of us here who hasn't come to understand the meaning of the cross, what it means that Christ suffered and died on that cross for our sins, and that we owe our redemption to him. We owe our hope and assurance of eternal life with God in heaven to him. I know that Christ on the cross and his resurrection three days later are the only events that allowed me to be saved. Yet, even though I know all that in my head and my heart, how easy it is for me to forget about the cross. Just like I walked in here and left this metal cross in my locker, I do the same thing all too often with the cross of Jesus. It's just that easy for me to walk out onto that shop floor and get so wrapped up in some problem or whatever is going on that I forget the cross of Christ. I can forget who I am as a born-again follower of Christ. I can act stupid. I can act in ways that make Christ seem like a lie in my life instead of the source of my very life. How about you? Do you forget the cross? And how can we help each other keep from forgetting the cross?"

Hands went up all around, and intense discussion followed, with lots of honest confession and brainstorming of great ideas for keeping the cross at the forefront. By the time it was Jake's turn to speak again, the discussion had helped him to realize new things about himself. "Why do I have that new license plate on my truck, the one about God?" he asked, "Why do I keep all those Bible verses and sayings on my locker door? Why do I wear hats and tee shirts with Christian slogans? Why do I listen to Christian music at my work station? Why do I surround myself with so many Christian symbols and reminders all day long? And why do I like to have that cross on the table during these Bible study times? They all help me not to forget about the cross! And Lord knows, the kind of sinner at heart I am, I sure need these constant reminders!"

Everyone laughed, but they understood that Jake was speaking for them as well. As the study session ended with voluntary prayers, person after person asked God to help them remember the cross of Christ during every minute of every day. By the time they finished praying, the beginning of the official workday was just minutes away. All hands pitched in to get the room cleaned up, then scattered to reach their posts in the plant. Thanks to occasional reminders from the boss, everyone knew that even after three trouble-free years of the Bible study, he remained skeptical. They were still on probation.

As Jake and the other Bible study participants settled into their work, feeling fortified and encouraged by the morning's session, the boss headed down the corridor into the beat-up conference room, his top assistants and a delegation of potential new customers in tow, executives from a growing Asian company setting up its first American assembly facility. The boss hit the lights, his eyes darting around the room. Everything was just the way he liked it, neat and orderly, but obviously well used and a little on the worn side. That was the image he liked to portray to his customers. He liked his plant to be perceived as the no-frills, no-nonsense supplier of great products at fair prices, and he felt certain that the perception was about help him close a very lucrative deal with these buyers.

At that moment, the boss saw it—the humble cross at the center of the table. In his rush to get everyone back to work on time, Jake had forgotten the cross again. The customers saw it too, exhibiting obvious signs of unease and speaking urgently among themselves in their own language. The boss had personally courted these buyers, visiting their home country in the process, and he was well aware that their predominant culture and religion was averse to Christianity. Furious and embarrassed, he frantically tried to smooth over the blunder, ordering his assistants, "Put that cross away!"

The boss didn't know if he could save the deal, but he knew one thing for sure: *That's the end of that foolish Bible study! I never should have let this happen. I knew it would come back to haunt me. Tomorrow I'm shutting all that crap down. No more Bible studies. No more Bible talk. No more God clothing. No more God stuff on lockers. No more God stuff on cars in my lot. This has got to stop before it's too late. We can't run a global business by chasing off customers with crosses and Bibles!*

For Christians

Religious expression in the workplace takes many forms. For some, it is wearing a cross necklace or Christian necktie. For others, it may be tee shirts with Christian messages, listening to Christian music, or hanging religious artwork in an office or cubicle. Some people have lockers rather than offices, but they choose to express their faith by placing Scripture verses on their lockers. Others live out their faith by having a Bible study with coworkers at lunch.

Regardless of where we each work, we spend roughly twenty-five percent of our time there each year. When faith is a part of our lives, it is only reasonable that faith will be part of our work life, too. The same can be said for any other nonreligious activity and hobby. Regardless of whether we spend our free time reading the Bible, praying, gardening, exercising, eating, or sleeping, chances are we will discuss our activities with coworkers and supervisors in our workplaces. Chances are we will surround ourselves with things that reflect what is important to us.

A simple legal rule of thumb regarding religion in the workplace is that if an employer allows personal expression in the workplace, religious personal expression should be allowed, too. It is important to understand that private employers have the right to determine what they allow at their businesses. If private employers allow personal expression in individuals' workspace, that personal expression can be religious in nature. But if private employers prohibit posting of personal belongings, then they can usually prohibit religious items. The same general rule applies to conversations. If employees are allowed to discuss nonreligious matters in the workplace, it is perfectly legal for them to discuss matters of religion there. Employees of private organizations need to remember that the private business owners determine what is and is not allowed in the workplace, as long as they fulfill their legal obligation to make reasonable accommodation for sincerely held religious beliefs.

An employee is permitted to bring her Bible to work and keep it in her company vehicle or at her desk if she is compelled to do so by her sincerely held religious belief. However, it is the employee's responsibility to communicate her belief to her employer in order to provide the employer an opportunity to accommodate her religious belief or expression. This applies regardless of whether the workplace is public or private. A possible exception to this rule would be if safety dictates a requirement or prohibition: in other words, no personal items are allowed on the production floor. In safety-related instances, an employer could easily justify a prohibition on personal items of any type due to safety concerns.

When it comes to Bible studies at the workplace, the rule varies depending on whether the place of employment is public or private and whether company property is used for other nonwork-related activities. The law is quite clear concerning public employers due to a number of Supreme Court decisions that say if a public space is allowed to be used for secular purposes then religious activities also must be allowed. Certainly private employers have the option of prohibiting use of company facilities for any nonwork-related activities. But, if private employers allow facilities to be used for activities that are not work related, and only exclude religious activities, then those employers may have a legal problem. Furthermore, if an employee sincerely needs to pray during the workday, an employer must reasonably accommodate the religious employee's prayer time unless it creates an undue hardship.

Title VII, the law that governs workplace discrimination, including religious discrimination, prohibits "disparate treatment." Disparate treatment is when a person is treated differently than other people based on religious beliefs, practices, or observances. The reason for an employer treating one employee different than another may be bias against a particular belief or even a preference toward a particular religious belief. For example, some Christian employers allow "prayer breaks" during the workday. These breaks are similar to smoking breaks where an employee is allowed to step away from work for a brief period of time. If a prayer break is allowed for Christian employees, it would be unlawful to prohibit prayer breaks for Muslim employees. Doing otherwise would be an example of disparate treatment by showing a preference for Christian prayer. On the flip side, if an employer allows a smoker to take cigarette breaks but prohibits Christians from taking breaks if they pray or discuss Christianity, such disparate treatment against Christians is prohibited.

An employer cannot refuse to recruit, hire, or promote an employee because of his or her religious beliefs or nonbelief. The two possible exceptions are if the employer is a religious organization or religious school, or in matters regarding the hiring of a pastor, minister, or similar employee to convey the message of that particular faith. The Supreme Court in 2012 upheld this so-called "ministerial exception."[37] Employers must be fair to all employees, regardless of whether or not the employees are religious, and whether or not the employees have the same religious beliefs as their employers. A Christian employee has the right to be treated the same as other people, including in matters of religious expression. For example, if employees can hang a personal calendar in their workspaces, hanging a scriptural calendar would be fine, too. In fact, in a federal case where an employee sued her employer for not forcing another employee to remove religious sayings from her cubicle, the employer won! The court said, "An employer … has no legal obligation to suppress any and all religious expression merely because it annoys a single employee."[38]

Another area of frequent contention is clothing and grooming. A public or private employer must accommodate an employee's sincerely held religious belief regarding clothing and grooming, just like with religious speech or other displays of faith, unless such clothing and grooming causes an undue hardship. Safety concerns, universally

---

37 Hosanna-Tabor Evangelical Lutheran Church & School v. Equal Employment Opportunity Commission, (132 S. Ct. 694, 2012).

38 Powell v. Yellow Book USA, (445 F. 3d 1074, 2006).

considered to be undue hardships, are almost always exceptions to accommodation requirements. For example, refineries and chemical plants require everyone who enters the property to be clean shaven. This is because a respirator may be required in the event of an emergency, and beards can prevent a respirator mask from sealing properly. It is unlikely that such employers would be required to accommodate a religious practice that forbids men from shaving their facial hair. However, public image or customer preferences usually fail the undue hardship test. Likewise, assumptions are not reasonable evidence of undue hardship; actual evidence of hardship is required. Simple fear of offending a customer is not a valid reason to refuse accommodation for an employee's sincerely held religious belief or practice.

What if a person's religious expression actually does offend other people? Federal courts have determined that a balance must be reached between the religious employee and the business. One such example involves an employee's religiously motivated view of abortion. An employer who allows employees to post personal décor in their cubicle or office does not have to allow items that are offensive. A bumper sticker that reads, "My mom chose life," may be deemed appropriate but it is possible that a graphic photograph of an aborted baby may be considered off-limits by a reviewing court.

Displays that are in view of the public may be restricted if a patron might attribute the display to the business rather than to an individual employee. Prohibitions on items that would disrupt the workplace, create hostility, or demean other people are usually within the law. A lunchroom or locker room not open to the general public would likely have a lower standard than a reception area. Rules against offensive displays apply to the workplace, not to an employee's personal vehicle even when it is parked on company property.

Demands to remove religious bumper stickers or other religious displays from a personal vehicle would probably constitute religious discrimination. If the dress code allows for casual Fridays when employees can wear jeans and tee shirts, Christian tee shirts with Scripture or other religious words or symbols should be allowed, too. If an employee can wear a tee shirt featuring a sports team, favorite vehicle, or superhero, a Christian tee shirt cannot be forbidden without violating the law.

As Christians, we should always seek to glorify God in what we do and say at home, work, and the community. We must strive to be good witnesses in the workplace, not just by the religious clothing or jewelry we wear, or what we put on our office walls, but by our conduct and work ethic. As the saying goes, we may be the only Bible someone ever reads. Let's make it count!

Quick Counsel for Christians

★ Religious expression is perfectly acceptable in the workplace.

★ Prohibitions on religious speech during nonworking hours such as breaks, lunch, or before work are usually unlawful.

★ Employers can allow Bible studies, Scripture reading, and prayer during the workday as long as participation or attendance is not mandatory.

★ If company property is used for nonwork activities, a Christian cannot be excluded from that same space merely because the activity is religious.

★ If conversation on secular subjects such as sports or family is permitted during the course of the workday, religious conversation should be permitted, too.

★ Employers avoid disparate treatment claims when they follow the same standards for religious and nonreligious activity.

★ Just because one employee is annoyed by overt religious expression doesn't mean that all vestiges of religion must be removed from the workplace.

They've Crossed the Line...

Everywhere Else

You Want to Do What At the Park?
Public Property and Facilities

Tear Down Those Commandments!
Displays and Monuments

No Ministry In Our Backyard!
Zoning and Land Use

The Tyranny of the Sensitive?
Holiday Displays

Shut Up!
Abortion Protests and Pro-Life Voices
of Silent Victims

Chapter 11

You Want to Do What at the Park? Public Property and Facilities

The newly constructed local government center gleamed, set tastefully into the rolling topography of its generous and elaborately landscaped hillside lot. Katie parked her minivan in the freshly paved and striped parking area below. After the usual ten-minute process of unbuckling and reorganizing her toddler twins from their car seats into their stroller, she pushed slowly up the long, winding, concrete sidewalk to the building, sweating in the hot afternoon sunshine. As the automatic entry doors opened, she was grateful for the cool air conditioning inside.

A new resident in the community, Katie was impressed as she looked around the spacious lobby of the municipal campus. *I am glad we chose to live inside the city limits*, Katie thought as she scanned the building directory for the department of parks and recreation. *Even though things seem a little more expensive and the taxes are kind of high, services and amenities for residents are so great, and everything is kept up so well—first class all the way!*

Arriving at the department's office, Katie was greeted by a friendly, middle-aged woman who seemed genuinely glad to see her. From behind a low marble counter, the woman cooed over the twins and then asked politely how she could be of service.

"You know that big beautiful park down by the waterfall, with those nice, new, picnic pavilions?" Katie asked, to which the woman nodded happily. "Well," Katie continued, "I'm embarrassed to tell you I don't actually know the name of the park. We only just moved here a few months ago, and I am interested in reserving a pavilion."

The woman smiled warmly and reached for a form. "It's Veterans Memorial Park, of course, and welcome to Liberty Falls. We are delighted to have you living here! And, oh, by the way, my name is Janet." Sliding the form and a pen toward Katie, she added, "Now, let me check the reservation calendar while you start filling out this simple application form. Don't worry, it's easy, just some basic information and our liability waiver to sign—you know, the usual legal stuff."

As Janet turned to her computer, navigating to the master schedule for the town's extensive recreational facilities, Katie started filling in the form. As she completed it, Janet asked, "What date do you want the pavilion?"

"June 15," Katie replied.

"Fine," Janet said, typing information into the calendar. "Pavilion number three is still open for that day. Honestly, I think that's the nicest one—best view of the falls. I'll mark you right in and then get you a confirmation slip. Let me see your form please so I get the correct spelling of your name." Katie handed her the form. "Very good.... Katie Evanson... E – V – A – N – S – O – N," Janet stated slowly, deliberately tapping in each key as she spoke. "You're all set...."

Janet's voice then trailed off, and her cheerful expression evaporated as she focused intently on Katie's form. "What's wrong?" Katie asked. "Did I make a mistake?"

"Um...," Janet stammered, "ah... the 'intended use' box. I'm looking at what you, uh, wrote there. I don't think... I don't know if.... Excuse me," Janet stated, ducking toward an adjoining office suite. "I'll be back."

Standing at the vacant counter with her twins, Katie tried to remember exactly what she had written in that box.

As best as she could recall, she had jotted the words "evangelistic outreach for area youth" or something close to that.

Katie and her husband, Colin, had moved to Liberty Falls as commissioned, domestic youth missionaries, sent and supported by their home church in another state. They were expected to fully integrate into their new community by working part time, preferably in local middle and high schools, to earn part of their income and provide a natural, social framework for building relationships with the young people they were to serve. Although a prosperous upscale community like Liberty Falls might have seemed like an unconventional choice as a mission field, it had been carefully picked because demographic data showed an unusually low and rapidly decreasing percentage of self-identified Christians in the area.

So far things had worked out very well. Colin, a standout varsity athlete in college, did lots of substitute teaching in physical education and landed a junior-varsity, football coaching position at the high school. Katie worked as a cafeteria server early mornings in the free, hot breakfast program one of the middle schools offered for its small group of lower-income students.

For their evangelistic outreach at the picnic pavilion, Katie and Colin planned to provide a big pile of food and invite a number of local kids they'd been meeting to bring along their friends. After fun games and activities, they would offer a simple Gospel message of salvation. She and Colin had trained to do this, and it would be the first big step in building the relational foundation they had worked hard to nurture and establish. Certainly there wouldn't be anything illegal or inappropriate taking place in the park, and Katie pondered what triggered Janet's odd reaction to the simple description of intended use.

Katie could hear muffled, animated discussion coming from the adjoining office suite, but could not understand specifics. At one point, new voices joined the conversation, and she distinctly heard a loud male voice say, "She wants to do what at the park?"

More than fifteen minutes later, Janet returned, clutching Katie's application and accompanied by a younger man not much older than Katie. "Ms. Evanson, this is Rob Woodlawn, our Director of Parks and Recreation," Janet stated stiffly.

"Pleased to meet you, Ms. Evanson," the man said, extending a hand to Katie. She shook his hand tentatively, saying "Yes, it's nice to meet you too, Mr. Woodlawn. What's going on? What's the problem?"

Rob smiled broadly and began a lengthy explanation, but in a roundabout style that left Katie even more confused. Finally she felt compelled to interrupt. "Are you saying we can't use the pavilion because we plan to talk about God at our picnic?"

Rob and Janet made brief eye contact, then almost simultaneously said, "Excuse me, we'll be right back."

Again Katie found herself alone with the twins, who were becoming restless. *Wow, this is getting weird,* Katie thought. *I wish Colin were here.*

Janet and Rob returned with a tall, older man, distinguished in appearance and very assertive. As he began to speak, Katie recognized his voice as the loud one she overheard earlier. "Ms. Evanson, I am Harold Filberton, solicitor for the city of Liberty Falls," he began in a lecturing tone. "I have a great deal of experience and a vast working knowledge with regard to the law, and I can assure you unequivocally that the policy you are questioning is squarely within the parameters of applicable legal precedent in this great state."

"But Mr. Filberton," Katie interjected boldly, "I don't even know what policy you're talking about. All I did was fill out the form. I didn't question the policy, I just asked Mr. Woodlawn a question, the same question I'm going to ask you now:

Are you saying that we can't use the pavilion because we plan to talk about God at our picnic?"

Mr. Filberton cocked his head and contorted his lips. "That may be your characterization, Ms. Evanson, but it would not be an accurate representation of the circumstances." He leaned down closer to Katie's face. "The determination is one resting upon far more subtle and weighty considerations. It is our duty, as expressed in our policies, to respect the rights of all of our citizens. And one of our paramount purposes in the administrative application of our policies is to avoid endorsement or approval of any activity within our jurisdiction that would tend to encroach upon those rights."

The twins were squirming, and Katie became increasingly uncomfortable with Mr. Filberton intruding into her personal space. She stepped back and shouted, "Enough!" The monologue ended. "Enough," she repeated firmly, "I don't need your legal mumbo jumbo. I'm not a lawyer like you, and I don't understand fully what you are trying to say. But I think you are telling me that if I had written 'picnic' or 'games' or 'youth activities' on that form, there would have been no problem, but because I used the words 'evangelistic outreach' you are not going to let me rent the pavilion."

Mr. Filberton shook his head disdainfully. "Again, I dispute your characterization," he stated, turning to Janet and Rob as if needing sympathy. They shook their heads gravely, affirming him. Katie, exasperated, spun the stroller abruptly and left the room, striding toward the exit.

The three officials watched for a moment, then Janet said, "That's the last thing we need in this town—religious fanatics taking over our parks. I'm glad I read that form before I confirmed her reservation."

"Yes, excellent work," praised Rob, looking relieved. "Excellent."

"But I'm not so sure we've seen the last of her," the attorney cautioned. "Consult me immediately if she returns.

These crazies can be awfully persistent, especially when they believe their 'god' is on their side."

Counsel for Christians

"Congress shall make no law...abridging the freedom of speech" states the First Amendment to the Constitution. But this prohibition is not just limited to the federal government. Through the Fourteenth Amendment, free speech applies to state and local governments as well. The right to freedom of speech is not absolute, though. As mentioned previously, a person can't yell "Fire!" in a crowded theater. Certainly public safety is a valid government concern justifying some appropriate legal restriction of the right to speak freely. Likewise, courts have held that some types of speech can be forbidden, such as obscene speech. But the Constitution severely restricts the government's ability to prohibit private speech when the reason is because of the speaker's viewpoint or the content of the speech.

The legality of content-based restriction depends on where the desired speech is occurring and what the basis is for the restriction. If the location of expressive activity is a public park, street, or sidewalk the government's speech restrictions are extremely limited. A complete ban of the freedom of speech in a public park is unconstitutional. In the 1939 case, *Hague v. CIO*, the Supreme Court expressed a very restrictive view of the government's power to control speech on public property such as parks, streets, and sidewalks: "Wherever the title of streets and parks may rest, they have immemorially been held in trust for the use of the public and, time out of mind, have been used for purposes of assembly, communicating thoughts between citizens, and discussing public questions."

Places such as parks, sidewalks, and streets are what are known as "traditional public forums" according to the

Supreme Court in a case titled *Perry Educational Associa-tion v. Perry Local Educator's Association*. Although the gov-ernment can't outright ban all speech in a traditional public forum, it can implement narrowly limited restrictions. In the "quintessential public forum" or place where people have always had the freedom to express their views, *Perry* explains it like this:

> For the State to enforce a content-based exclusion it must show that its regulation is necessary to serve a compelling state interest and that it is narrowly drawn to achieve that end... The State may also enforce regu-lations of the time, place, and manner of expression which are content-neutral, are narrowly tailored to serve a significant government interest, and leave open ample alternative channels of communication.

So, it is important to understand that a complete ban is illegal, but time, place, and manner restrictions in a public park are okay. They just cannot be arbitrarily content based. A city cannot completely ban a church, youth group, or evan-gelistic speaker merely because the speech is *religious*.

What possible compelling government interest could legally justify restricting *all* religious conversation at a public park? Some city leaders might argue that a so-called com-pelling reason to totally prohibit religious speech in a public park is the desire of these officials not to offend other citizens. Or, they might say they don't want to appear to be endorsing religious views. The mere fear of offense, however, does not trump the First Amendment!

Traditional public *fora* restrictions on speech must be *rea-sonable* regarding time, place, and manner. But what does "reasonable" mean anyway? Restrictions must be narrowly tailored to serve a compelling or major government inter-est. But that's not all; there must also be *ample* alternatives regarding the religious speech. A regulation that states a person can't amplify music or the speaker after 10:00 p.m. would be reasonable. Or, putting restrictions on where in the park the event can be held would be reasonable from a public safety standpoint.

Other type of time, place, or manner restrictions that have been held constitutionally sound are licensing or permitting requirements. Licensing often involves an application process, possibly the payment of a fee, and approval of the application. All of these restrictions are fine as long as they are implemented in a nondiscriminatory fashion.

A government cannot speak or act except through its designated human agents. Some person or group of people has to have the delegated authority to approve or deny a permit on the government's behalf. Usually a government administrator or employee is charged with approving such applications. That, in and of itself, is not a problem. However, it becomes a problem if the government grants too much discretion to that person in the approval process.

Approval or denial cannot be based on the content of the speech. For example, a regulation that requires a permit for any assembly over fifty people is probably content neutral. Such a regulation makes sense in light of the limited amount of space available in a particular location. A permit process that requires a written application will also seem reasonable, particularly if a written policy spells out any advance notice requirement and gives a time frame for approval or denial. A designated appeal process would probably be helpful to prove reasonability of a time, place, or manner restriction.

An example of a regulation that would likely be *unconstitutional* would be one that ties the cost of the permit to the content of the speech. For example, a regulation charging a higher fee for a controversial speaker because the listeners' actions will probably require more police presence is likely to be unconstitutional because the listener's reaction to protected First Amendment activity should not determine the speaker's cost to exercise his or her right to freedom of speech. Such a rule would basically punish a speaker financially based on the content of the speech, which would exemplify an unconstitutional, content-based restriction. To survive a constitutional challenge, a regulation must be content neutral; government cannot grant access to a public place by granting a permit or license when the government agrees with the subject or viewpoint, and deny access when the government disagrees with the subject or viewpoint.

Unfortunately some local municipalities, in an overzealous effort to assure the perceived separation of church and state, erroneously believe that it is a compelling government interest to avoid religion in public. In the 1981 case, *Widmar v. Vincent*, the Supreme Court specifically addressed the issue of promoting separation of church and state by forbidding religious speakers in a public forum. The Court determined that the alleged compelling interest was not compelling enough to justify religiously based discrimination. The Establishment Clause is balanced by the Free Exercise Clause. Whether at risk because of a perceived threat of lawsuit by groups like the ACLU, or outright hostility toward religion, religious speech is a protected, First Amendment right.

Another area of similar concern involves public facilities other than parks, streets, or sidewalks. For example, many local park and recreation departments have community rooms where various neighborhood activities occur. Governments may choose to allow people to use these facilities, subject to various rules and regulations. Often these facilities require an application, payment of a fee, or even proof of citizenship within the particular city or county. These community rooms are not necessarily a traditional public forum; they are government property that municipalities have chosen to open for public use. Another familiar example would be a school classroom or cafeteria that the school has opened up for public use after school hours or on weekends. The government can stop allowing the public to use this facility at their discretion, therefore these community rooms likely qualify as a limited or designated public forum. One legal caveat to closing such a forum is that the government's decision cannot be for discriminatory reasons. The government cannot suddenly choose to close a limited forum as a means of avoiding access to those whose content is found to be objectionable.

The legal standard for government restriction of speech in a limited public forum is nearly the same as for a traditional public forum. Legally acceptable restrictions of protected First Amendment activity in a limited public forum must be content-neutral time, place, or manner restrictions. Content-based restrictions must be narrowly tailored to a compelling government interest. Other acceptable government regulations on expressive activity in a limited public forum are permitted as long as they are viewpoint neutral and reasonable in light of the location's purpose and use.

An example of a content-neutral time, place, or manner restriction would be a rule that music and singing are not allowed during a specific time period when a meditation class meets next door. But if the restriction is that no *religious* music and singing is allowed during a given time, that would be an unlawful viewpoint-based restriction on protected activity. If a youth activity is permitted at a community facility, as long as it isn't an *evangelistic* youth activity, that would be content-based discrimination and violate the Constitution.

Quick Counsel for Christians

★ Parks, public streets, and sidewalks are places where the freedom of speech is highly protected; they are known as "traditional public forums."

★ The government can place reasonable time, place, or manner restrictions on private speech as long as it is content neutral. A noise ordinance is such an example.

★ A restriction based on content must be narrowly tailored to promote a compelling government interest. "Separation of church and state" is *not* a compelling government interest in the context of free speech!

★ Free speech is not without limits, though; i.e. government can prohibit obscene speech or speech that incites a panic.

★ Acceptable forms of content-based restrictions include license or permit requirements as long as the administrator does not have too much discretion in approving or denying a request.

★ If the fee for a license or permit is determined by the level of controversy of the speech, it is probably unconstitutional.

★ Religious groups *can* use public facilities under the same reasonable terms and conditions that apply to nonreligious users.

Chapter 12

Tear Down Those Commandments! Displays and Monuments

E ighty-year-old Whitfield Belmont sat silently in the far corner of the back row in the empty courtroom gallery. He still remembered sitting in the very same spot as a young boy, more than seventy years ago, during the official dedication ceremony for the new courthouse. Squeezed uncomfortably between his mother and father, he had watched as the curious, small-town crowd filled the room to capacity. He remembered how the judge and county dignitaries rose in turn, each praising the workmanship of his grandfather, a master craftsman in wood and plaster who sat beaming in the front row, enjoying the prime of his life and the pinnacle of his success. Whitfield also remembered how a town clergyman led a prayer of dedication and afterward the entire assembly recited the Ten Commandments, reading them enthusiastically from the massive new courtroom wall that Whitfield's grandfather had just completed. At this exhilarating moment, Whitfield first experienced the mature awareness of God that eventually drew him toward faith in Jesus Christ and a committed Christian life.

The skillful artistry of his grandfather, evident throughout building's interior, was revealed most notably by that spectacular, eye-catching, floor-to-ceiling portrayal of the Ten Commandments that dominated the courtroom, its words inset deeply into the thick plaster in a unique and elegant script. *How many defendants and plaintiffs, witnesses, jurors, judges, lawyers...,* Whitfield wondered, *were inspired to integrity during these past seventy years by those powerful words? How many people did the right thing in this courtroom thanks to my dear grandfather's masterpiece? How many were drawn to God?*

Obviously Whitfield's grandfather was long gone now, as were his mother, father, and every local luminary who stood and spoke in the courtroom during that dedication ceremony. Back in those days, a judge had risen to publicly praise and honor his grandfather's masterpiece, not only for its artistic value but for its meaning, content, and beneficial relevance to the grave judicial proceedings that would unfold in the courtroom. Now, seven decades later, the latest in a long line of new county judges—a judge born, educated, and elevated to the bench in an era of militantly secular legal theories—intended to rip the law by its roots from the rich soil of Judeo-Christian morality in which it sprouted. Presiding in this same courtroom, with the Ten Commandments still bold and immovable on the wall at his back, this judge ordered the county to tear down the wall containing the Ten Commandments.

Whitfield was shocked when he first heard word of the judge's order. Over a picture of the robed judge sitting smugly at his bench in front of the mighty wall, a local newspaper headline blared, "Tear Down These Commandments!" Few area residents had paid attention when an obscure, out-of-town law firm quietly helped to prepare and file a lawsuit on behalf of a local atheist who claimed his civil rights had been violated during his recent divorce litigation by the presence of the Ten Commandments in the county courtroom. Nothing had been reported about the lawsuit until the order was issued. And by the time Whitfield read the headlines, it was too late.

Alarmed by the news, Whitfield contacted the aging remnants of his once-large network of faithful friends and acquaintances, trying to round up help and financial support to hire a lawyer and appeal the judge's order. Although some people expressed sympathy, nobody seemed interested enough to make a contribution to the cause. He wrote a letter to the editor of the newspaper, hoping to encourage others to come the aid of the imperiled Ten Commandments, but there was no response. Whitfield grew discouraged by the indifference. "Times have changed, Whitfield," people told him. "We have to live in today's world." A few letters even appeared in the paper supporting the judge's ruling.

In the end, Whitfield had to tap his modest retirement savings to hire a young lawyer who did her best to overturn the ruling but lost the appeal. "The standard of review was too difficult to overcome," she explained. "Maybe if we had intervened earlier, we could have placed necessary evidence on the record to support our position, but now I don't see much chance for a successful result. All we have left is an appeal to the state supreme court, and based on what you told me I don't think you have the kind of money to pay me for that." Sadly, she was right. Whitfield couldn't afford to spend more money on legal fees.

As he sat in the empty courtroom pondering and remembering, Whitfield felt very alone. He carefully read aloud through the Ten Commandments on the wall for what he believed would be the last time, tears blurring his vision by the time he reached the bottom. He heard the bell of an old nearby church strike the hour and knew it wouldn't be long now, *It's probably just a few minutes before the demolition crew from the county's remodeling contractor arrives*, he thought, *and begins tearing the plaster and the sacred words it contains from this great wall.*

Suddenly the courtroom doors flew open, and a jovial crew of three young men in their twenties clattered in, dressed in paint-covered overalls and carrying ladders and tools. The men set right to work taping a big, clear, plastic sheet across the entire front portion of the room. Whitfield wasn't sure they even noticed him sitting in the back until one of the men looked his way and said with a friendly grin, "Hey, old dude, you can stay and watch, but even with this sheeting it might get pretty dusty in here. That's some thick old plaster we're hacking into, and the dust will really be flying. Just fair warning." The man then slipped a dust mask over his face and ducked under the sheet into the work zone.

Whitfield nodded and stayed put. It was the only way he knew to honor the memory of his grandfather, to bear silent witness to the destruction of his legacy. And, Whitfield was beginning to fear, perhaps he would be bearing silent witness to the destruction of what little remained of God's influence on his culture.

The noise began, growing in intensity—hammering, cracking, sawing—as the workers unleashed their arsenal of tools against the mighty relic of God's holy words. A light covering of fine, white dust drifted from behind the plastic, settling over Whitfield and everything else. He looked at the backs of his hands, now almost ghostly in their whitish coating. "Lord," he prayed, "I'm not only starting to feel like an ancient ghost, I'm starting to look like one. Help me, Lord, to live out my days in this upside-down world in a way that reflects your glory."

Several hours later, the men completed the demolition. They pulled down the sheeting, exposing the wall stripped down to bare timbers and beams. Dusty rubble and chunks of lath and plaster lay heaped on the floor. "See ya, old dude!" the worker shouted to Whitfield as the three men headed for the exit. "Hope you enjoyed the show. We'll be back after lunch for cleanup."

Whitfield stood slowly, whisking dust off his head and sleeves, and shuffled his way to the debris. He didn't know what he was looking for, but he looked anyway. There, amidst the chips and broken plaster, he saw a thick slab, more than a foot long, with the word "love" perfectly intact. "Hmmm," he said, bending over to reach it.

It was heavy, at least for a man his age, but Whitfield hefted the plaster onto his shoulder and left the courtroom. In the hallway, a sheriff's deputy working security saw Whitfield carrying his burden and approached him with a mix of caution and concern. "Sir, can I assist you with something?".

"No, that's all right, young man," Whitfield answered, smiling for the first time all day. "I think I know what God wants me to do now. I think God has answered my prayer. He will answer your prayers, too! Now please have a wonderful day!" Then Whitfield left the courthouse and lurched his way down the sidewalk toward his favorite restaurant, carrying his strangely tangible expression of God's love. *I feel almost like a latter-day Moses coming down off Mt. Sinai with inscribed tablets of stone,* Whitfield thought. *I may not have been able to save the Ten Commandments on the courthouse wall, but no judge can take God's love away from me! Even as a tired, old man, I can still bring that love to people! And for today, this chunk of my grandfather's plaster will sure make it easy for me to start telling more people about God!*

Counsel for Christians

The latest attack on this nation's Christian heritage and the moral foundation of the law and our legal system has occurred in the form of attacks on displays, mottos, seals, and monuments all over this country. The first of many challenges occurred in 1980 in the case, *Stone v. Graham*,[39] which challenged a Kentucky state law requiring the posting of the Ten Commandments in every classroom in every public school in the state. The Supreme Court applied the *Lemon*

---

39 Stone v. Graham, 449 U.S. 39 (1980).

test,[40] which states that in order for government action to be constitutional it must: 1) have a secular purpose; 2) have a principal effect that does not advance or inhibit religion; and 3) must avoid excessive government entanglement with religion. The Court determined that there was no secular purpose and therefore found Kentucky's law, and the posting of the Ten Commandments, unconstitutional.

Nearly twenty-five years later, on June 27, 2005, the issue was decided regarding different Ten Commandment displays. It was a bizarre day indeed. The Supreme Court handed down not one, but two decisions involving public displays of the Ten Commandments. The problem with the decisions is that they reached opposite conclusions! The cases were *McCreary County v. ACLU of Kentucky*[41] and *Van Orden v. Perry.*[42] Each involved a display of the Ten Commandments on public property and whether the displays violated the Establishment Clause of the First Amendment. Remember, the First Amendment prohibits government establishment of religion.

McCreary involved three attempts by two counties in Kentucky to erect Ten Commandment displays in the county courthouses. (After all, the Ten Commandments are the foundation of our legal system.) The Court struck down the displays as unconstitutional establishment of religion. In so doing, the Court relied on the *Lemon* test (secular purpose, neither advancing nor inhibiting religion, and no excessive government entanglement).

The second case, *Van Orden*, involved a Texas Ten Commandment display that was part of a larger permanent display on the capitol grounds. The Court referred to the nature

---

40 Lemon v. Kurtzman, 403 U.S. 602 (1971).

41 McCreary County v. American Civil Liberties Union of Kentucky, 545 U.S. 844 (2005).

42 Van Orden v. Perry, 545 U.S. 677 (2005).

of the display and the political and legal history in determining that the display did not violate the Constitution. Imagine, the highest Court in the United States came out with two decisions, on two cases, on the *same* constitutional issue, on the same day, but with two different results. To complicate matters further, since then some courts have used a later-developed test, the so-called "endorsement test," rather than the *Lemon* test. Lower courts all over the country are coming up with different conclusions using nearly the same facts!

Perhaps Justice Scalia best described the sorry state of Establishment Clause law in his concurring (he agreed) opinion in *Van Orden*. He wrote, "I join the opinion of the Chief Justice because I think it accurately reflects our current Establishment Clause jurisprudence—or at least the Establishment Clause jurisprudence we currently apply some of the time." One lower court described the confusion after *McCreary* and *Van Orden* by stating, "We remain in Establishment Clause purgatory."

The motto of the Supreme Court is "Equal Justice Under Law." The Supreme Court is charged with the duty of interpreting the U.S. Constitution. All other courts in the country must follow the laws as the Supreme Court has interpreted them in cases. Each time a particular issue comes up, no matter where in the country and regardless of the varying details, every court should follow these same rules. But if the rules are so confusing that even federal judges can't understand them, how on earth can officials from the local civic league, city government, or public school understand what they can and cannot do?

The Supreme Court hears only about 150 of the thousands of cases it is asked to decide each year. The process of asking the Court to decide a matter involves filing a Writ of Certiorari, which is essentially a formal request for a case to be heard. Then, in a confidential process, the justices decide which cases to hear. Recently Justice Thomas wrote a nineteen-page dissent because he disagreed with the Court's decision to *not* take a case in order to clear up confusion concerning monuments and displays. The case involved the placement of memorial crosses along the highway in Utah to memorialize fallen officers. Justice Thomas described the law on the constitutionality of religious displays on government property as "anyone's guess." He wrote, "It is *this* Court's precedent that has rendered even the most minute... details of a religious display relevant to the constitutional question. We should not now abdicate our responsibility to clean up our mess because these disputes, by our own making, are 'factbound.' It is a sad day indeed when a justice on the Supreme Court describes a particular area of law as "anyone's guess."

Since *Van Orden* and *McCreary*, many lower courts have used the *Lemon* test; others have used the endorsement test. Still others have used the historical and political history method from *Van Orden*. One court followed the *Lemon*/endorsement and *Van Orden* in the same case! Justice Thomas used many of the nineteen pages in his dissent to point out specific instances throughout the country when different courts have reached different decisions on very similar facts using what the Supreme Court says is the law.

Justice Thomas observed that the endorsement test has taught us that a nativity or crèche on government property "violates the Establishment Clause, except when it doesn't." And a menorah on government property "violates the Establishment Clause, except when it doesn't." Further, "A display of the Ten Commandments on government property also violates the Establishment Clause, except when it doesn't." Finally, a cross erected on government property (you guessed it) "violates the Establishment Clause, except when it doesn't."

The Supreme Court has answered questions about religious displays in different ways, depending on the *very* specific facts of a given case. Consequently, the average person, city official, or school principal often decides to err on the side of caution and not permit *any* public religious displays. But that too can be a constitutional violation if it is solely the religious nature of the display that results in denial by a decision maker!

It seems there are no easy answers and no clear test(s), so the best we as lawyers can do in anticipating the outcome of future legal challenges is to consider someoverarching generalities, such as an apparent judicial distinction between inside and outside displays. Those outside are more likely to be found constitutional. Likewise, the length of time a particular display or monument has been up seems to give a greater chance of surviving a constitutional challenge. The intent or purpose seems to be more significant than the perception of observers, though what conclusion a reasonable observer would make as to whether the government was endorsing a particular religion is nonetheless important. A temporary display tends to be viewed more favorably than a permanent one, though permanent monuments that have not had much notice or ceremony for decades seem more likely to survive.

Context is very important, too. Often monuments displayed in a reasonably equal manner with other symbols of other faiths are likely to be acceptable to the courts. It is still constitutional to acknowledge the role of religion in the life of society, American history, and the law. The guiding principle would appear to be the context in relation to other items of significance being highlighted by a particular display or monument. Is the monument passive, or does it compel the passerby to read, meditate or reflect on the content of the message? A passive display is likely more acceptable in the eyes of the courts. A religious message that applies to more than one faith appears more palatable to the courts than a specifically Christian symbol, such as a picture of Jesus. Again, the nuances are very specific to the entire factual circumstance. Nonetheless, it is probably more likely that a longstanding monument or display could be justified whereas a newly erected religious symbol may be more problematic under legal scrutiny.

In February, 2009, the Ten Commandment case, *Pleasant Grove City v. Summum*,[43] was decided. The interesting difference between this case and most others involving the Ten Commandments was that it was not an attempt to *remove* a monument on Establishment Clause grounds but rather attempted to force a city to *install* a monument in a public park based on freedom of speech grounds. The park in question had more than a dozen monuments, including a donated Ten Commandments monument. The Summum church argued that since the city accepted the Ten Commandments monument, it had to accept theirs, too.

The Supreme Court decided unanimously that Pleasant Grove City could not be forced to accept and install a donated monument. In free speech cases, the government cannot discriminate against private speakers based on the content or viewpoint of the speaker. However, the same does not apply to government speech. The Ten Commandment monument, though privately donated, became government speech when the government accepted and installed the permanent monument in the city park. Therefore the rights of an individual to freedom of speech did not apply in that case because it was deemed government speech.

Quick Counsel for Christians

★ These cases are *very* fact specific. All of the circumstances must be assessed to evaluate whether there is an Establishment Clause problem with a specific display or monument.

---

43 Pleasant Grove City v. Summum, 555 U.S. 460 (2009).

★ Different courts in different parts of the country have come up with different results using the same Supreme Court cases to support their decisions.

★ Just because a monument is religious doesn't automatically mean it must be removed from display in public as a violation of the Establishment Clause. New monuments may not be treated the same way, however.

★ Municipalities *can* often keep religious displays, like the Ten Commandments, when they are part of a larger display that conveys the history of law, society, or American history.

★ Important concerns are: context, content, purpose, proximity, and temporary or permanent status.

Chapter 13 ✯ No Ministry In Our Backyard! Zoning and Land Use

R ich couldn't believe his alarm was going off already. He'd had a tough time falling asleep, tossing and turning on his thin floor mat all night. Finally he dozed off at 3:00 a.m. Now it was 6:30, time to get everyone up and moving. He was tempted to snooze, sneaking just five more minutes of rest, but he knew the importance of being the example and leading with his actions. Getting to his feet, Rich flicked on the lights, prompting a chorus of groans. "Wake-up call!" he shouted, his voice gravelly. "This is the day the Lord God has made, let us rejoice and be glad in it! Time to pack up, clean up, and roll on out!" He forced himself to smile.

Rich was pretty sure he heard outright cursing mixed with the general grumbling his announcement inspired, but at least people were moving. The men had slept on his side of the church's all-purpose room. On the other side, beyond an extended room divider, the women stirred, too. Waking up a roomful of homeless people wasn't the glamorous vision of ministry Rich had in mind when he first accepted God's call to become a pastor, but now, with fifteen years of church leadership under his belt, he sensed that serving the homeless was at the very center of God's mission for him and his congregation.

After three weeks, the routine for operating the modest, emergency homeless shelter within Community Faith

Church had already become fairly predictable for Pastor Rich and his crew of dedicated rotating volunteers. At 9:00 each night, Rich and his shelter team would open the church doors, do a brief intake interview with each guest (mostly to screen out anyone who might be intoxicated or was wanted by the police), assign each person a mat and clean bedding, and then lead them in a brief Bible study followed by time for individual prayer and counseling. Lights out was strictly enforced at 11:00 p.m., and everyone had to help with morning clean-up before leaving the building by 7:00 a.m. The accommodations were not fancy, but for the homeless guests it was far better than the dangers and discomforts of sleeping on the street, especially on nights when the weather was nasty.

The church was small and restroom facilities were limited, so the trustees had set the total nightly capacity for the ministry at only sixteen guests. *Yeah*, Rich realized, *it's just a drop in the bucket compared to the entire homeless population around here, but sixteen people still receive Christ's loving hospitality and a Gospel message of hope.* And that, Rich believed, was why his church existed.

As gray morning clouds signaled another cold raw day, Rich escorted the last guests onto the sidewalk and returned to lock the church door. He had just enough time to get home for a quick shower and coffee before a busy day of ministry responsibilities. As his key clicked the lock, someone yelled angrily, "There's Pastor Rich! He's the one behind all this! Let's let him know how we feel!"

On cue, a group of a dozen or so grim-faced people carrying large signs began chanting, "Not in our neighborhood! Not in our neighborhood! Not in our neighborhood!"

Their signs were emblazoned with slogans such as "Keep our streets safe!" and "Our kids live here—not druggies and bums!" and, most troubling to Rich, "Real Christians respect their neighbors!"

As the chants grew louder, passing commuters started blasting their horns and giving thumbs-up signals through their car windows in solidarity with the bitter protesters. Rich stood there trying to grasp the situation, asking himself who and why.

Suddenly he recalled tossing away an anonymous letter he'd recently received from someone who claimed to live in the neighborhood. The letter demanded, in the most colorful and threatening language imaginable, that he shut down the shelter immediately. Rich had dismissed the communication without much thought since there was no name attached to the complaint. *Maybe I should have viewed that letter as a sign to work harder at reaching out to our neighbors*, he second-guessed, watching as more people streamed from every direction to join the protest.

Whatever mistakes he had made, he couldn't ignore this escalating crisis. He prayed for God's help and felt led to try to engage with the protestors meekly and humbly. His hands trembled as he approached the hostile crowd.

With the target of their protest now in their midst, the organized chants of the protestors degenerated into angry slurs and jeers. Rich tried to pick out a leader, someone to talk with in a rational way to defuse the anger, but the crowd seemed more interested in insulting him than conversing with him. His optimism faded, as did his hope for initiating productive dialogue, when a local television news crew rolled up to the scene to broadcast a live report. This prompted a new burst of intense chanting and sign waving as protestors played for media attention.

Discouraged, Rich shuffled back to the church and knelt in the chapel to pray about the unexpected confrontation unfolding in the neighborhood. As he prayed, Rich's thoughts began to clear. Deciding to convene an emergency meeting of the church's board of elders, he started making cell-phone calls, telling each elder about the protests, the television coverage, and his concerns about what might happen next. "We've got to get together to pray and plan," he told each one, "It's urgent!"

As Rich updated the last elder, the church doorbell buzzed. "Listen," he said, "I'll call you back if I can, but it's best if you just head over here. Someone's at the door now, probably an angry neighbor. Pray for me to say and do the right thing."

To Rich's surprise, a calm, well-dressed man carrying a clipboard and displaying an identification badge stood there. The protestors were now smiling and cheering. "I'm Ryan Dominick, codes enforcement officer," he announced, "here to serve you with this cease-and-desist notice." Pushing a paper firmly into Rich's hand, the man continued as the crowd burst into applause and celebratory whoops. "As you see by the text of this notice, your church is hereby ordered by the codes department to cease and desist from any further operation of your unlawful use of these premises as a homeless shelter, which is not a use permitted under our zoning ordinance anywhere within this district of our municipality."

The codes officer then hopped into the passenger seat of what appeared to be an unmarked police cruiser, which sped off as the crowd roared. *Who or what do they think we are?* Rich thought, *We're just a simple church trying to care for people of this community. Are they really so afraid of us that they needed to send the codes officer over with a police escort? And can they really make us stop running this ministry? This church has been here for fifty years. How can they suddenly decide it's illegal for us to perform a Christian ministry? Isn't that what we're here for? Isn't that what a church does?*

Rich made copies of the notice and distributed it to the arriving elders. When all the elders assembled around a table in the all-purpose room, he talked about the morning's events, including his rebuffed attempts at peacemaking. He also shared his misgivings about the way in which he had handled the anonymous letter and asked them to join him in a time of earnest confession and prayer. "Once we've confessed our failings and shortsightedness," he added, "then we can figure out our next steps."

Counsel for Christians

Can hostile governments shut down church ministries using local zoning and land use laws? "Congress shall make no law respecting an establishment of religion or prohibiting the free exercise thereof" reads the First Amendment to the Constitution. But what does "prohibiting the free exercise" really look like in light of the modern proliferation of zoning and land use laws and regulations? The Civil Rights Act of 1964, although enacted most notably to address racial discrimination, included legal protection for religion right alongside race, color, sex, and national origin. Congress deemed it necessary even though the First Amendment's dual religion clauses already protected citizens from domination by a government sponsored national church and protected our freedom to worship freely without persecution.

Religious freedom court cases from the 1960s established a test that courts could use to determine if a government law burdened the free exercise of religion. This test arose out of the case, *Sherbert v. Verner*.[44] There, the Supreme Court set forth the two-part analysis that *if* a sincerely held religious belief was substantially burdened by a particular law, *then* the government would have to prove that it had a compelling interest in order to lawfully burden a person or group's religious exercise. Also, the government would have to prove that the particular law provided the least restrictive way to do it.

The 1980s began a new era regarding the free exercise of religion when cases brought forth a new rule that if a law or

---

44 Sherbert v. Verner, 374 U.S. 398 (1963).

action by the government "incidentally burdened" religion such a law or action was acceptable, even if the "incidental burden" completely banned a particular religious practice. This era culminated in the 1990 Supreme Court decision in *Employment Division v. Smith*[45] that said free exercise did not mean individuals were exempt from valid, religiously neutral laws even if the law or regulation substantially burdened free exercise of religion. The *Smith* decision outraged the public This new interpretation was entirely different than the previous practice! If a law or regulation was generally applicable to all people, it was permitted even when it infringed on religious freedom. This meant that state and local governments could pass a law that did not *overtly* burden religion on its face, but nonetheless had the same effect of hampering religious freedom. Thus a decade-long tug-of-war began between the Supreme Court and Congress.

Congress responded to *Smith* by passing the Religious Freedom Restoration Act (RFRA) in 1993. This Act served to prevent laws that would substantially burden a person's free exercise of religion. This included churches, schools, and other ministries, not just individuals. RFRA provided that religiously neutral laws that burdened free exercise of religion had to pass "strict scrutiny." (Remember, that means a compelling government interest by the least restrictive means.) So, once again the courts would essentially have to follow the former test set out in *Sherbert*: a law had to meet the criterion of advancing a compelling government interest by the least restrictive means possible. This was how Congress attempted to legislate around the Supreme Court.

It worked, but only for a short time—and only in reference to the federal government. In 1997 the Supreme Court ruled that RFRA was unconstitutional as applied to the fifty states,

---

45 Employment Division, Department of Human Resources of Oregon v. Smith, 494 U.S. 872 (1990).

although it still applies to federal laws, because it was not a proper exercise of Congressional power. The new case law said that laws of general applicability were fine even if they substantially burdened religion, as long as they furthered a compelling government interest in the least restrictive way possible.

The next step on the journey for Congress to rein in the Supreme Court on religious liberty was to find a legislative remedy for the free exercise of religion that would restore the strict scrutiny standard for state and local governments, too. So, Congress held nine hearings focused on religious discrimination between 1997 and 2000. Consequently Congress found "massive evidence" of blatant and indirect religious discrimination in two areas: zoning and land use decisions and institutionalized persons. Some cities banned all churches; other cities banned churches from using existing buildings such as movie theaters that were used previously for public assemblies. Congress discovered that this religious discrimination was often subtle and veiled behind issues such as traffic, design, or master planning.

Congress discovered that there is practically unlimited discretion and virtually no objective criterion in zoning and land-use decisions. Because of the convergence of the limitless discretion and subjective standards, Congress found this area rife with religious discrimination. The solution was the *Religious Land Use and Institutionalized Persons Act* (RLUIPA) that restored the strict scrutiny standard to review adverse land-use decisions. In 2000, the House and Senate passed RLUIPA unanimously.

RLUIPA prohibits government—federal, state, or local—from imposing land-use regulations that place a substantial burden on the religious exercise of individuals, assemblies, or institutions unless there is a compelling government reason and it is the least restrictive means of achieving that interest. Furthermore, governments cannot pass land-use regulations that treat religious groups or institutions on less-than-equal terms than nonreligious ones. And, governments cannot completely exclude religious institutions from a particular city, county, or town, nor can a particular belief system be excluded.

Incidentally, because Congress found that institutionalized persons also suffered from religious discrimination, they were included with the land-use legislation. For example, some institutions prohibit patients/inmates from having Bibles. Frequently, due to the vast amount of discretion that prisons, jails, juvenile detention centers, and psychiatric facilities have, religious liberty violations occurred. Religious discrimination claims by institutionalized persons now also require strict-scrutiny judicial review under RLUIPA. However, the Supreme Court has held that prisoners cannot seek monetary damages for violations, unlike those in the land-use arena who can sue for monetary compensation.

Even after RFRA and RLUIPA, there are still issues yet to be resolved. Some of these relate to a church's activities outside of normal Sunday services. Some churches, for example, provide a clothing-closet ministry through which they minister to the needy within their communities by providing free clothing. Or, churches want to provide a food pantry for feeding the hungry or have a vision for a homeless outreach that provides a place to sleep inside the church or on the church grounds. Such ministries often meet opposition, particularly if a church is in a residential neighborhood. Many courts around the nation have grappled with the delicate balance between deciding if a particular land use is a "religious exercise" while trying to steer clear of making a judgment about a religious organization's method of ministering to its congregation and community. Some courts have questioned whether homeless ministries are in fact "religious exercise." In some states, the answer is an emphatic, "Yes!" For example, a New Jersey judge conveyed disbelief in *St. John's Evan-*

gelical Lutheran Church v. City of Hoboken[46] when he wrote, "Any inconvenience to the City of Hoboken and its other residents pales into insignificance when contrasted with what the occupants of the shelter would have to face if turned out into the city streets in winter weather." Many churches view feeding the hungry, clothing the needy, and giving shelter to the homeless an integral part of the exercise of religion.

Other courts around the country have issued a resounding, "No!" Many of these cases involve churches' and ministries' refusals to even apply for permits or zoning variances. Courts nationwide are fairly consistent in denying the ability to completely forego the application process. Yet these discrepancies between different states and localities make it difficult to understand exactly what a church can and cannot do.

Add to this a nationwide discrepancy about what "substantial burden" really means. Some churches have easily shown that a complete prohibition on serving the homeless is a substantial burden on their religious exercise because it is inappropriate for courts to determine whether a particular ministry or practice is an integral part of that group's religious exercise. Churches can easily point to Scripture and history to support the contention that helping less-fortunate people has been a function of the church since time immemorial. The ability of the local church or ministry to reach out to the homeless is often viewed as a way to interact with that segment of the community, thereby offering help and Christian charity. Even so, churches that have a long history of food-distribution programs or allowing the homeless to sleep in or on church property often have an easier time showing a substantial burden when the government attempts to shut down or prohibit these programs.

---

46 St. John's Evangelical Lutheran Church v. City of Hoboken, 479 A.2d 935, 939 (N.J. Super. Ct. Law Div. 1983).

Quick Counsel for Christians

★ The Free Exercise clause of the First Amendment provides Constitutional protection for religious practices.

★ There is further protection via the *Religious Land Use and Institutionalized Persons Act.*

★ Like so many religious liberty issues, these cases are *very* fact specific. All circumstances must be assessed in order to evaluate whether or not there is a Free Exercise problem or if an RLUIPA violation exists.

★ Different courts in different parts of the country have come up with different definitions for the "substantial burden" and "equal terms" provisions of RLUIPA.

★ Substantial burden is more than an inconvenience, but churches do not have to prove that there is no other place within that locality to conduct their ministry.

★ Equal terms means that nonreligious assemblies cannot be treated better than religious ones.

★ Most courts around the country require churches to at least apply for permission to use church property for expanded ministries just as any other landowner or business would be required to do.

★ Zoning ordinances cannot completely exclude religious assemblies.

★ A substantial burden to religious exercise triggers the government's duty to show how the particular rule is in furtherance of a compelling government interest and is the least restrictive means of doing so. Mere complaints from neighbors are not sufficient to claim a compelling government interest.

★ The U.S. Department of Justice Civil Rights Division can enforce RLUIPA.

★ RLUIPA includes places of worship, religious schools, prayer meetings, and the like in private homes and faith-based social services such as food pantries, homeless shelters, and group homes.

Chapter 14

The Tyranny of the Sensitive? Holiday Displays

T he Community Improvement League was a loosely organized group, bound together more by tradition than by rules and formalities. Its members held meetings just twice each year, and the league's budget was next to nothing. The only planning and fundraising its members did was focused strictly on providing basic logistics for the two ongoing projects they sponsored—setting up and taking down two modest, annual holiday displays in the small public courtyard on the historic town square.

For more than 150 years, the league had coordinated these traditional displays, one for Independence Day and one for Christmas. The formula was simple. On set-up day, league volunteers used a borrowed truck (in the early years it was a borrowed farm wagon) to bring display components out of storage and unload them on the square. With the help of many supportive, local residents who always came forward to assist, league members quickly set up the displays and then after the holiday packed them up for maintenance, repair, and storage until the next year.

League members understood that their organization wasn't the hardest working or most important one in town. Many other charities and civic groups were tackling bigger community needs and more challenging tasks. Yet what the league accomplished, in its own small way, was woven into the very fabric of local life and culture, part of the heart and soul and spirit that made the community an exceptional place to live and raise a family.

The July 4th display was, of course, patriotic and utilized many flags and a small-scale mock-up of Independence Hall. The Christmas display featured a nativity scene and included flood-lighting for night-time illumination. Neither display was particularly elaborate, but both were beloved local traditions. There wasn't a kid in town whose parents didn't insist on snapping their pictures in front of the displays, pictures that were often lined up on mantles or shelves alongside pictures of their parents and grandparents as children taken in the same poses so many years ago.

For Leanne Simpson, being elected president of the league this year was a highlight. It wasn't the kind of group in which members campaigned for the top jobs. In fact, even though such jobs didn't provide any perks or benefits, if people made it too obvious that they wanted those jobs that usually generated enough suspicion about their motives to cause members to vote for other people. Attaining presidency of the league was considered a genuine recognition of the winner's humble character, evidence that everyone liked and trusted this person to do what was right. *Winning the presidency,* Leanne thought, *means that I follow in the footsteps of my deceased mother, grandfather, and great-grandfather, all of whom served honorably as president of the league.* So, Leanne enjoyed a special sense of connection with each of these deceased relatives, especially her mom, who she still missed very much.

In early December, Leanne drove to the old barn where the displays were stored to ensure everything was in order and ready for Christmas. She remembered coming to this same barn for the same purpose as a little girl, tagging along with her mom. She always treasured this early Christmas memory. Now, as she looked over the neatly organized materials, her eyes filled with tears, pining for her mom but treasuring the privilege of carrying on the tradition across so many years and generations.

Although the town was small and the area still fairly rural, the community was by no means isolated or naive. People had full access to the latest technology and communications, and everyone was well aware of the annual "Christmas wars" that seemed to flare up in the news every December—the controversies over retail employees wishing customers a "merry Christmas" versus a "happy holiday," disputes over whether public-school choirs could ban the singing of Christmas carols during their "winter" concerts, and the court battles over the placement of nativity scenes on public property. Even so, all that controversy seemed remote, fights that other people were having in other places. No one ever expected the Christmas wars to arrive on their quaint town square.

On a cold, crisp, December evening, members of the Community Improvement League and friends cheerfully put the final touches on their classic nativity scene. They made sure the lights were placed just right, paused for the customary Christmas blessing by a local pastor, and posed for a smiling group photograph before departing for warmer gathering places. None of them noticed the silently seething man peering down on them from his attic apartment just off the square.

Gordon Rinchler's tiny efficiency apartment had only two windows, one of which directly faced an adjoining brick wall. The other window, though, provided him with a picturesque view of the town center. He would often sit in front of this window, day after day, reading in his worn-leather chair. Other than taking short daily walks to get exercise and provisions, Rinchler spent virtually all his waking hours by that window, devouring book after book. Since his arrival in town late last summer, his attitude and demeanor had immediately established his reputation as a cranky, eccentric loner.

Most people who saw him assumed he was poor, and his haggard face and rough, old clothes suggested that he might even be a drifter of sorts, someone used to surviving on the road.

In reality, Rinchler was a burned-out litigation lawyer on the run from decades of intense, exhausting, day-to-day legal combat in a high-powered, big-city practice. Toward the end, he had lost a string of cases he knew he should have won against what he perceived were lesser foes. He attributed his failure to the effects of advancing age and the loss of the vital mental edge on which he had always relied to win. So, he decided to withdraw from the field of battle rather than be humiliated there. He came to this simple country town to live out his days "off the grid," as he cryptically informed his former partners the day when he suddenly and unexpectedly departed from the law firm.

Rinchler's litigation practice had earned him lots of professional recognition and even more money, but it had cost him everything. By the time of his retirement, he had been divorced twice and become completely estranged from his children and grandchildren. In fact, he had transformed himself so thoroughly into the ruthless tough guy he liked to portray for his clients that he had no close relationships with anyone. Alone, he often found himself overcome with hostility, ready to lash out indiscriminately. Books seemed to provide his only refuge from anger, and all he wanted to do now was sit and read—alone. He chose the barest of accommodations and amenities because he no longer cared about luxuries or anything else. All he asked from his vast material wealth was the ability to keep buying books.

During the early years of his practice, though, when he was still striving to make a name for himself and earning his reputation as a notoriously fierce advocate, Rinchler especially enjoyed serving as a "pro bono" volunteer lawyer for his city's branch of the National Civic Freedom Front (NCFF).

Founded by a group of radical leftist academics in the late 1960s, the NCFF had an expressed goal of erasing the presence and influence of religion from the public life of the United States. That goal had seemed audacious and outlandish at the beginning, but now, decades later, the NCFF had proven to be more effective than even its founders could have imagined. Rinchler had been a big part of that success, winning case after case for NCFF clients, establishing legal precedents that made it harder and harder for citizens to exercise their religious liberties in the public square. As a lifelong atheist, he believed this was progress, something beneficial for the country. Although he hadn't volunteered much for the NCFF during the latter years of his career, he remained deeply sympathetic to its goals.

Consequently Rinchler became agitated to his core as he watched members of the Community Improvement League and their merry volunteers arrive at the public courtyard beneath his window and set up the nativity, their joyful work ritual punctuated with so many smiles and friendly hugs. For the first time since retirement, Rinchler could feel the stirring of his former killer instinct, the consuming drive that powered him to survive and conquer so many courtroom adversaries over so many years. He wanted to knock the joy off their faces. He wanted to get that nativity scene off the public square and out of his view. And he knew just how to accomplish it.

It isn't just their religion, he realized as he punched in the telephone number for his previous law firm, *it is their audacity that infuriates me. How dare these people set up a Christian Christmas display right in middle of the town square? How dare they ignore law and common sense? How dare they impose their primitive religion on me? What century do they think they're living in?*

Rinchler knew that attorneys at the law firm would be working late into the night, especially the younger associates, because they always did. They had no choice if they expected to make the cut. It was part of the game at that level—nights, weekends, holidays, always more to do, never an acceptable excuse to avoid the office. So, it wasn't long before Rinchler was talking with the lawyer he wanted, an aggressive young woman following in the footsteps of his own early career. Already a rising star, she was a favorite pro bono attorney of NCFF insiders.

By 3:30 the next afternoon, Rinchler was on the local county courthouse steps, meeting a private courier sent by his new lawyer and bringing the fruit of her all-night labors. The courier handed him emergency legal pleadings spelling out demands for a preliminary court order to immediately ban the nativity from the public courtyard. "Gordon Rinchler vs. Leanne Simpson" was the official caption of the case, although the Community Improvement League, all its officers and members, and the municipal and county governments were also included as defendants.

Rinchler had won many cases like this and, he was sure, he would win this one too, only now as the client rather than the lawyer. He raced inside the courthouse, striding toward the clerk's office to officially file the lawsuit, unable to hold back a smile as he envisioned the scenes of fear and distress that would soon unfold as local sheriff's deputies served all those arrogant Christian townspeople with his early Christmas gift.

Counsel for Christians

The Christmas wars are still occurring each December! The most pressing question on most people's minds is whether a religious Christmas display, often one that has stood annually for many years, is allowed in a public place or even on government property. The short answer is: often yes, but it depends. The Supreme Court has answered this question in several different ways depending on the very specific facts. Perhaps more than any other area of First Amendment law, Christmas displays cause the most confusion. Frequently this confusion leads to overreaction which results in a Scrooge-like response that practically screams, "Bah humbug!" Yet, nothing in the Constitution or current Establishment Clause cases requires governments to sanitize Christmas (or anything religious) from public life. The key to legal acceptability is that a government policy on Christmas must be neutral; if it happens to benefit religion, that's not a problem.

"Congress shall make no law respecting an establishment of religion, or prohibiting the free exercise thereof." The actual text of the First Amendment to the Constitution applies to the federal government. But what about state governments? Or cities? Or counties? The 1947 decision in the case of *Everson v. Board of Education*[47] (a New Jersey controversy over reimbursement for parents transporting students to public and private school) was the first time the Court applied the Establishment Clause to the states via the Fourteenth Amendment. When a question arises on whether a public religious display is constitutionally prohibited, there must be some standard the courts will look to for guidance. Although the Supreme Court generally stated that "the Constitution doesn't require complete separation of church and state" in the 1984 case, *Lynch v. Donnelly*, the Establishment Clause cases actually provide the most guidance on how to tell if a government action on Christmas displays conforms to the Constitution.

In these cases, the Court has used three tests or approaches. The first is the three-part *Lemon* test, resulting from the 1971 Supreme Court case *Lemon v. Kurtzman*.[48]

---

47 Everson v. Board of Education of the Township of Ewing, 330 U.S. 1 (1947).

48 Lemon v. Kurtzman, 403 U.S. 602 (1971).

The *Lemon* test states that in order for government action to be constitutional, it must: 1) have a secular purpose; 2) have a principal effect that does not advance or inhibit religion; and 3) not cause excessive government entanglement with religion. But the *Lemon* test is not always followed. In fact, it seems the Supreme Court uses it when it suits its purpose and ignores it when it doesn't! Justice Scalia described the Court's invocation of the *Lemon* test this way: "Like some ghoul in a late-night horror movie that repeatedly sits up in its grave and shuffles abroad, after being repeatedly killed and buried, *Lemon* stalks our Establishment Clause jurisprudence...frightening the little children and school attorneys.... Its most recent burial...was, to be sure, not fully six feet under."

The second potentially applicable test is referred to as the "endorsement test." Justice O'Connor created this test in *Lynch v. Donnelly*.[49] She explained that government can potentially violate the Constitution either by endorsing or disapproving of religion: "Endorsement sends a message to nonadherents that they are outsiders...and an accompanying message to adherents that they are insiders ... Disapproval sends the opposite message."[50] Thus, under the endorsement test, a government action is constitutionally invalid if it is intended to or has the effect of either endorsing or disapproving a religion. The courts use this test, which focuses on neutrality toward religion, alone or in conjunction with the excessive entanglement prong of the *Lemon* test.

The third test is the "coercion test" found in the 1992 decision, *Lee v. Weisman*.[51] This test focuses on assuring that no one will be coerced by government action to support or participate in a religious exercise. Unfortunately there is no

---

49 Lynch v. Donnelly, 465 U.S. 668 (1984).
50 Id. at 688.
51 Lee v. Weisman, 505 U.S. 577 (1992).

consensus among the nine justices of the Supreme Court on which test to use in which situation, hence why it is difficult to determine how the Court would rule under any given set of specific circumstances.

To further complicate matters, in addition to the afore-mentioned tests rooted in the Establishment Clause, the judicial perspective on the constitutionality of a religious display is also guided by *who* owns the display and *who* pays for it to be put up, taken down, and lighted; *what* is displayed with it, or if it is alone; *where* the display is located; *when* it is displayed and for what time period; and *how* it is displayed. These factors all relate to the key question of what type of "forum" is involved. The Supreme Court, in *Perry Education Association v. Perry Local Educators Association*,[52] estab-lished three types of forums: traditional public forums, des-ignated or limited public forums, and nonpublic forums. The traditional public forum is a place that has traditionally been used for the public such as streets, sidewalks, and parks. This forum offers the greatest First Amendment protection. In contrast, the limited public forum is a place the government has opened for expressive conduct to occur. Once opened up, the government must apply neutral standards for any content-based limitations on speech. Both traditional and limited public forums require the government to prove a compelling reason for any actions curtailing the content of speech. Such limitations must be narrowly tailored to suit that compelling interest for a content-based restriction to be constitutionally imposed. There can be reasonable time, place, and manner restrictions on speech, however. A non-public forum can be completely restricted for public use. Just because the government owns a particular property does not mean the public automatically has access. For example the

---

52 Perry Education Association v. Perry Local Educators' Association, 460
    U.S. 37 (1983).

government, without further explanation, can forbid access to military bases. It is important to note that a limited public forum can be transformed into a nonpublic forum as long as it is done in a neutral manner.

Within the framework of all that legal background, three primary cases currently guide the courts in determining whether a public Christmas display meets constitutional muster. The first is the 1984 case, *Lynch v. Donnelly.*[53] There, the Court analyzed the circumstances in a very fact-specific manner, and it applied both the *Lemon* and endorsement tests. The case involved a crèche that was part of an outdoor holiday display that included reindeer and sleigh, a Santa Claus house, a Christmas tree, lights, candy-striped poles, carolers, and a sign that read "Season's Greetings." The Court held that the crèche was part of a wider holiday display that depicted the history and origin of the national Christmas holiday. Viewed in that context, the Court concluded that the crèche was constitutionally permitted.

The second case came five years later, in *County of Allegheny v. ACLU, Greater Pittsburgh Chapter.*[54] This case involved two displays: one indoors at the courthouse and the other outdoors at the city-county building. The indoor display was only a crèche; the outdoor display had a Christmas tree, a sign saluting liberty, and a large menorah. Viewing each display separately, the Court evaluated the very specific set of facts in concluding that the crèche was unconstitutional but the menorah was not. Because the crèche was the only display at the grand staircase of the county courthouse, a place not open for anybody else to put up displays, and was accompanied by a Latin sign translated, "Glory to God in the Highest," the Court determined a reasonable person would

---

53 Lynch v. Donnelly, 465 U.S. 668 (1984).

54 County of Allegheny v. American Civil Liberties Union, Greater Pittsburg Chapter, 492 U.S. 573 (1989).

think that the government endorsed the display. In contrast, the menorah was to be viewed in the context of the greater display that portrayed a secular message.

The third case, *Capitol Square Review & Advisory Board v. Pinette,*[55] was heard in 1995. It answered the question whether an unattended, privately owned decoration placed in a public square adjacent to government buildings violated the Establishment Clause. The case involved an application to place a cross, "an unattended religious symbol," in the square; the Board argued that the close proximity to government buildings would violate the Establishment Clause. The policy regarding who could place items there was religiously neutral. The Court found that it was a traditional public forum, in contrast to the courthouse staircase in *Allegheny,* and further stated, "Our precedent establishes that private religious speech, far from being a First Amendment orphan, is as fully protected under the Free Speech Clause as secular private expression." The key difference between *Pinette* and *Allegheny* was what type of forum existed. Because the square in *Pinette* was a traditional public forum, the ability of the government to lawfully censor private speech was sharply curtailed and the cross could be displayed. But because the courthouse staircase in *Allegheny* was a nonpublic forum, the display of the crèche violated the Establishment Clause.

Other Christmas Issues

Unfortunately displays are not the only area of confusion regarding religion during the Christmas season. Private businesses and employers *can* lawfully include religion in their celebration of Christmas. They can, for example, require the use of a particular greeting by employees answering

---

55 Capital Square Review & Advisory Board v. Pinette, 515 U.S. 753, 760 (1995).

telephones, or the wearing holiday garb They may sponsor holiday parties, and they may put up religious decorations. An employer will run afoul of the law, however, if an object- ing individual is punished for not participating or is forced to participate. Reasonable accommodations must be made for objecting employees.

Public schools *can* allow Christmas carols as part of a choir or Christmas program that includes secular songs or other religious songs, too. Public schools *cannot* ban teach- ers and students from saying, "Merry Christmas" because they have individual rights to freedom of speech or expres- sion. Religious decorations and even reading the biblical story of Christ's birth aloud are also constitutional if there is a legitimate secular purpose such as educating about the cultural or historic meaning of the holiday or as part of a comparison of religions.

Quick Counsel for Christians

★ These cases are *very* fact specific. All circumstances must be assessed to evaluate whether there is an Establishment Clause problem with a specific display.

★ Different courts in different parts of the country have come up with different decisions.

★ Municipalities *can* erect Christmas displays, including religious ones, when such displays are part of a larger holiday display that includes a number of other elements.

★ Municipalities *can* allow individual access to government property for the purpose of displaying holiday displays, even if they are religious in nature,

★ Individuals *can* place religious displays on government property because individuals have free exercise and free speech rights that the government doesn't.

★ Private displays do not have to be part of larger secular displays as long as the criterion for choosing who is allowed to use the space is neutral. It's also best to include signage that removes any doubt as to whether the religious display is the government's.

★ Municipalities *can* exercise reasonable time, place, and manner restrictions.

Chapter 15 ✦ Shut Up! Abortion Protests and Pro-Life Voices of Silent Victims

Halfway through their first semester at Central Christian College, freshman roommates Sarah and Hannah became the closest of friends. Both young women, barely eighteen, were filled with the same high-energy idealism about how they could impact the world for Christ. But, both were experiencing the dawning realization that their lives up to now had been sheltered from many harsh realities of the twenty-first century. Listening to chapel speakers at their college turned out to be a transformative wake-up call for both of them. They learned shocking details of violent persecution of the worldwide church, horrors of human trafficking and modern-day slavery, ravages of extreme Third-World poverty, and now, tonight, the ugly realities of the abortion industry.

Walking back to their dorm, Sarah and Hannah grieved together over the inhuman pain that abortion inflicts on so many babies and women around the world, even right in their own community. "I don't think I really understood what was so wrong, so evil about abortion," said Sarah, her voice shaking with compassion, "until we saw those new high-resolution videos tonight of those innocent babies in the womb. How beautiful, delicate, and sweet they are, from the very beginning, and what a gruesome and agonizing death abortion puts them through."

Hannah agreed, tears running down her cheeks. "We've got to do something to protect those babies, Sarah. We have to! How can we even call ourselves Christians if we just stand by and let these precious little ones get murdered! We have to defend them!"

Neither girl could fall asleep. They talked, prayed, and finally in the early morning hours agreed on a plan. "We might be just two naïve college kids," Sarah exclaimed. "We might not be part of any big powerful groups or organized strategies, but we've got the downloads of those videos and our tablet computers. If we can at least get one woman who is about to kill her innocent baby to stop and watch, maybe we can get her to change her mind!"

"You are right!" shouted Hannah. "It's time for us to answer God's calling, to speak out for those who have no voice! We can't be silent!"

By early the next afternoon, Sarah and Hannah had found the local abortion clinic, a low-profile storefront in a declining part of downtown. The deceptive name "Family Health Center, Inc." was stenciled on the plate glass of its heavily draped front window. Hannah parked her car on an unmetered side street, and both women prayed, hand-in-hand, before walking hesitantly toward the clinic.

As they approached the center, a scruffy-looking man shuffled into their path and asked for spare change for bus fare. Sarah responded apologetically, "I'm sorry, Sir. We forgot to bring change. Well, we didn't forget, really, we just didn't even think about it. We are not used to parking in the city, so we had to park over there where there aren't any meters. But if you need a ride in a couple hours, we can drop you off somewhere... ." Sarah trailed off as the man, shaking his head dismissively, moved on. She and Hannah looked at each other and shrugged, then continued on their way.

At the sidewalk in front of the clinic, the women stood awkwardly, not sure what to do next. The neighborhood was almost deserted, with an occasional passerby on the sidewalk and a few cars on the street. After a few minutes, a man pulled his car to the curb and, leaning out the window, asked suggestively, "How much, ladies?" Sarah and Hannah answered, almost in unison, "For what?" The man shook his head and screeched away.

"That's weird," said Hannah, "He had the same reaction as that other guy. They just shake their heads at us and leave. The people here must not like us for some reason."

Sarah and Hannah turned in unison at the sound of the clinic door swinging open and a teenage girl and older woman walking toward them.. "Don't stare," Hannah whispered, tugging Sarah's arm.

"I won't," Sarah whispered back, "but should we say something?"

Hannah nodded, then tried politely to attract the pair's attention by raising her hand in a friendly wave and saying, "Excuse me, excuse me, could I show you something?"

The older woman, who Sarah and Hannah assumed was the girl's mother, scowled and answered gruffly, "I ain't buying nothing today, honey." The teenager said nothing, shooting them an icy glare.

As the pair walked away, another car, old and rusty with a loud belching exhaust, pulled up along the curb. A young couple got out, grim faced and silent, and the man put change into the meter. Hannah and Sarah's hearts pounded with anxiety. "This is it," Hannah whispered to Sarah.

This time, determined not to be ignored, they stepped forward boldly, getting between the couple and the clinic doorway. "Hi guys," Sarah announced, "I'm Sarah, and this is Hannah. We're students from Central Christian College and wondered if we could just talk to you for a minute?"

"What for?" the man said impatiently, "we're already late."

Hitting *play* and thrusting the screen of her small computer toward them, Sarah continued, sputtering a bit from nerves, "We were just hoping you could, um, watch this video please before you go in there. There's some things about the baby...."

As the word "baby" crossed Sarah's lips, the man smacked the computer, nearly knocking it out of Sarah's hand. He yanked the woman toward the clinic doorway, pushing forcefully past Sarah and Hannah. "You get that out of my face and stay away from us!" he yelled as they went inside, slamming the door behind them.

Inside, the clinic staff apologized to the couple. "We get these crazies all the time down here, these anti-choice fanatics trying to scare our patients," one staffer explained, "but don't worry, they'll be gone by the time your procedure is finished. The cops are already on their way to pick them up. We've been watching on closed circuit, and we've got everything on the surveillance tapes. This one is going to be easy, a slam-dunk prosecution."

Sarah and Hannah hadn't noticed the strategically arranged array of security cameras aimed at the sidewalk where they stood. The clinic, long accustomed to confrontations with pro-life activists, had taken every possible measure to fight back, including the state-of-the-art security system. Video evidence, the clinic had discovered, was often especially useful to the team of sophisticated lawyers they kept on call. Sarah and Hannah, novice sidewalk counselors who had no training or experience and no clue that there were special legal rules for speaking out against abortion clinics, would be easy targets.

As clinic staffers talked inside, Sarah and Hannah gave each other a pep talk, trying to overcome their shared disappointment at the way they were ignored and rebuffed on their mission of mercy. When two police cars rounded the corner and stopped in front of the clinic, for a fleeting moment both women imagined that perhaps justice was finally being done, that the cops were going to bust the clinic for all the horrors it had inflicted. But when the police ordered them both to the rear of their cars, read them their rights, and placed handcuffs on their wrists, it became obvious that something had gone dreadfully wrong.

"But wait," Sarah cried, "what about the Constitution, the First Amendment? I just studied it in my political science class. We have freedom of speech!"

One policeman replied, "Not here you don't. It looks like you violated the one-hundred-foot protest rule and the ten-foot buffer rule. You're heading downtown."

"But what about my car!" Hannah pleaded. "It's still over there in the alley." The police looked at each other knowingly, and the other said, "Don't worry, down here it won't last the night. And you seem like nice girls, so let me give you both some advice. From now on, just shut up."

One policeman guided Hannah into the backseat of his car; the other policeman did the same with Sarah. Both policemen then placed the young women's computers and phones in plastic bags, along with their purses.

Counsel for Christians

In 1973, the Supreme Court set the legal stage for the horrific and sustained purge of more than fifty-four million unborn children. This slaughter of innocents, on a historical scale exceeding Hitler's mass exterminations and approaching in magnitude the vast carnages of Stalin and Mao, continues today under the Court's unspeakably misguided legal protection. Pro-life researchers at LifeNews.com report an average of 3,300 abortions each day in America since 1973, or 137 abortions every hour.

Yet the number of abortions has begun to decline in recent years thanks to tireless teaching and family-support efforts by so many faithful pro-life advocates (and also to astonishing technological advances that allow more pregnant mothers to recognize the full and miraculous humanity of their tiniest unborn children). The bloody legally sanctioned rampage against babies in their mothers' wombs rages on, however. As voices of the pro-life movement grow in effectiveness, so do the sustained legal efforts of the abortion industry to silence them.

To understand the current legal landscape concerning attempts to restrict people's rights to speak out against abortion, and especially the attempts to prevent people from offering the hope of life to pregnant women considering abortion, let's start with that notorious 1973 Supreme Court decision, *Roe vs. Wade*.[56] In that tragic case, the Court declared that constitutional rights to privacy and liberty permit a woman to kill a baby growing in her womb. Amazingly, the Court cited no actual provisions of the U.S. Constitution to establish such rights, but rather relied on its belief that "zones of privacy," including what it called the "fundamental right" to abortion, must be legally protected.

From 1973 to 1992, the *Roe vs. Wade* case was the controlling legal authority, and the pro-life community and elected lawmakers could do little to lawfully resist the ensuing epidemic of abortions. Only a "compelling state interest" could legally justify any laws limiting the new fundamental right to abortion, a nearly impossible legal standard for abortion foes to meet. But in 1992, in the case of *Planned Parenthood of Southeastern Pennsylvania vs. Casey*,[57] the Supreme Court relented from the harsh "compelling state interest" standard, replacing it with a new, less-difficult-to-meet, "undue-burden" standard. So, laws restricting abortion are legally permissible unless they put an "undue burden" on a women's right to kill her unborn child. Disturbing and repulsive as

---

56 Roe v. Wade, 410 U.S. 113 (1973).

57 Planned Parenthood of Southeastern Pennsylvania v. Casey, 505 U.S. 833 (1992).

even that softer standard sounds, it has had the positive and practical effect of opening the floodgates of new pro-life laws in states across the country.

In 1994, feeling threatened by the growing successes of the newly empowered, pro-life community in saving the lives of unborn children, abortionists struck back with the passage of new federal legislation to restrict the right of pro-life protestors and sidewalk counselors to exercise free speech in areas near abortion mills. President Clinton signed the Freedom of Access to Clinic Entrances (FACE) Act (18 United States Code Section 248), into law, ostensibly to protect patients seeking abortions from threats of physical violence. Instead, the FACE Act has too often become a tool of government-sanctioned legal harassment and bullying of peaceful, pro-life sidewalk counselors.

The FACE Act, as it pertains to abortion clinics (that it euphemistically calls "reproductive health services") reads as follows:

(a) Prohibited Activities.— Whoever—

(1) by force or threat of force or by physical obstruction, intentionally injures, intimidates or interferes with or attempts to injure, intimidate or interfere with any person because that person is or has been, or in order to intimidate such person or any other person or any class of persons from, obtaining or providing reproductive health services;

***; or

(2) intentionally damages or destroys the property of a facility, or attempts to do so, because such facility provides reproductive health services...,

shall be subject to the penalties provided in subsection (b) and the civil remedies provided in subsection (c), except that a parent or legal guardian of a minor shall not be subject to any penalties or civil remedies under this section for such activities insofar as they are directed exclusively at that minor.

(b) Penalties.— Whoever violates this section shall—

(1) in the case of a first offense, be fined in accordance with this title, or imprisoned not more than one year, or both; and

(2) in the case of a second or subsequent offense after a prior conviction under this section, be fined in accordance with this title, or imprisoned not more than 3 years, or both;

except that for an offense involving exclusively a nonviolent physical obstruction, the fine shall be not more than $10,000 and the length of imprisonment shall be not more than six months, or both, for the first offense; and the fine shall, notwithstanding section 3571, be not more than $25,000 and the length of imprisonment shall be not more than 18 months, or both, for a subsequent offense; and except that if bodily injury results, the length of imprisonment shall be not more than 10 years, and if death results, it shall be for any term of years or for life.

(c) Civil Remedies.—

(1) Right of action.—

(A) In general.— Any person aggrieved by reason of the conduct prohibited by subsection (a) may commence a civil action for the relief set forth in subparagraph (B), except that such an action may be brought under subsection (a)(1) only by a person involved in providing or seeking to provide, or obtaining or seeking to obtain, services in a facility that provides reproductive health services...,

(B) Relief.— In any action under subparagraph (A), the court may award appropriate relief, including temporary, preliminary or permanent injunctive relief and compensatory and punitive damages, as well as the costs of suit and reasonable fees for attorneys and expert witnesses. With respect to compensatory damages, the plaintiff may elect, at any time prior to the rendering of final judgment, to recover, in lieu of actual damages, an award of statutory damages in the amount of $5,000 per violation.

(2) Action by attorney general of the United States.—

(A) In general.— If the Attorney General of the United States has reasonable cause to believe that any person or group of persons is being, has been, or may be injured by conduct constituting a violation of this section, the Attorney General may commence a civil action in any appropriate United States District Court.

(B) Relief.— In any action under subparagraph (A), the court may award appropriate relief, including temporary, preliminary or permanent injunctive relief, and compensatory damages to persons aggrieved as described in paragraph (1)(B). The court, to vindicate the public interest, may also assess a civil penalty against each respondent—

(i) in an amount not exceeding $10,000 for a nonviolent physical obstruction and $15,000 for other first violations; and

(ii) in an amount not exceeding $15,000 for a nonviolent physical obstruction and $25,000 for any other subsequent violation.

(3) Actions by state attorneys general.—

(A) In general.— If the Attorney General of a State has reasonable cause to believe that any person or group of persons is being, has been, or may be injured by conduct constituting a violation of this section, such Attorney General may commence a civil action in the name of such State, as parens patriae on behalf of natural persons residing in such State, in any appropriate United States District Court.

(B) Relief.— In any action under subparagraph (A), the court may award appropriate relief, including temporary, preliminary or permanent injunctive relief, compensatory damages, and civil penalties as described in paragraph (2)(B).

(d) Rules of Construction.— Nothing in this section shall be construed—

(1) to prohibit any expressive conduct (including peaceful picketing or other peaceful demonstration) protected from legal prohibition by the First Amendment to the Constitution;

(2) to create new remedies for interference with activities protected by the free speech or free exercise clauses of the First Amendment to the Constitution, occurring outside a facility, regardless of the point of view expressed, or to limit any existing legal remedies for such interference;

(3) to provide exclusive criminal penalties or civil remedies with respect to the conduct prohibited by

this section, or to preempt State or local laws that may provide such penalties or remedies; or

(4) to interfere with the enforcement of State or local laws regulating the performance of abortions or other reproductive health services.

(e) Definitions.— As used in this section:

(1) Facility.— The term "facility" includes a hospital, clinic, physician's office, or other facility that provides reproductive health services, and includes the building or structure in which the facility is located.

(2) Interfere with.— The term "interfere with" means to restrict a person's freedom of movement.

(3) Intimidate.— The term "intimidate" means to place a person in reasonable apprehension of bodily harm to him- or herself or to another.

(4) Physical obstruction.— The term "physical obstruction" means rendering impassable ingress to or egress from a facility that provides reproductive health services or to or from a place of religious worship, or rendering passage to or from such a facility or place of religious worship unreasonably difficult or hazardous.

(5) Reproductive health services.— The term "reproductive health services" means reproductive health services provided in a hospital, clinic, physician's office, or other facility, and includes medical, surgical, counselling or referral services relating to the human reproductive system, including services relating to pregnancy or the termination of a pregnancy.

(6) State.— The term "State" includes a State of the United States, the District of Columbia, and any commonwealth, territory, or possession of the United States.

Most recently, under President Obama's administration, the United States Department of Justice has wielded FACE Act prosecutions, and the threat of such prosecutions, to intimidate and discourage peaceful sidewalk counselors and demonstrators from exercising their rights to free speech in areas around abortion facilities. The legal threat to pro-lifers is very real, given the provisions in the Act providing for the imposition of large fines and even jail time. Numerous anecdotal accounts have been reported of highly questionable allegations and prosecutions for "assaults" on abortion clinic patients and staff that were, in reality, peaceful encounters, all of which has severe and chilling effects on those who would dare speak out for life near abortion mills.

In this hostile legal environment, anyone planning to peacefully protest or offer sidewalk counseling near an abortion facility should first obtain thorough training by knowledgeable advisors as well as solid, specific, legal guidance. The unpleasant reality is that these essential precautions are demanded during this challenging time in our nation's history, a time in which customary concepts of free speech rights have been severely curtailed. Although sidewalk counseling and demonstrating is still a constitutional right, a complex net of varying local laws could legally entangle even the most well-meaning pro-life people.

For example, in Pittsburgh, Pennsylvania, local laws establish so-called speech-free "buffer zones" within fifteen feet of abortion clinic entrances, and eight-foot, speech-free "bubble zones" around nonconsenting people within a radius of one hundred feet from any abortion clinic doors. To make matters more confusing, in the 2009 case of *Brown v. City of Pittsburgh*, the Federal Court of Appeals for the Third Circuit ruled that either the speech-free buffers or the speech-free bubbles could be enforced, but not both!

The most current, general, legal guidelines were set forth in the 1994 Supreme Court decision of *Madsen vs. Women's*

Health Center, Inc., which wrestled with the concept and application of speech-free zones. Importantly, the Court determined that no outright ban on sidewalk counseling or on the use of observable images or signs by pro-life protesters is permitted, recognizing that sidewalk counseling and protesting remain protected constitutional rights. The Court also reaffirmed that the constitutional right to free speech does not depend on the consent of the listeners. However, the Court then determined that the imposition of legally enforceable, speech-free zones on public sidewalks is permitted (although the Court noted that such zones on private property are not permitted) if access to the abortion clinic in question has been repeatedly blocked by unlawful obstruction in the past.

Although the courts have dismissed several recent prosecutions and requests for injunctions against pro-life sidewalk counselors (after vigorous defense by pro-life legal teams), caution and prudence are still strongly advised. The law governing these matters continues to evolve, sometimes in unpredictable or localized ways. Don't be intimidated into keeping silent, but know your rights and limits.

Peaceful pro-life picketing and protesting in the vicinity of abortion clinics are still legitimate, constitutionally protected activities. However, be sure not to stray into anything that could be interpreted as the use of force, the threat of force, or a physical obstruction. Sadly, the interpretation of what these terms mean by law enforcement officials can vary, depending on their political agenda. For example, during Obama's presidency, the pro-abortion Department of Justice alleged that the actions of an eighty-year-old, pro-life counselor who stood still on a sidewalk so that other people had to walk around him amounted to a violation of the FACE Act!

Unfortunately the battle over abortion-protest rights has been prolonged and is fraught with legal traps and pitfalls due to the sustained and aggressive pressure by abortionists and their allies. Pro-life advocates should be encouraged that their efforts to inform and educate are making a difference, saving thousands and thousands of precious lives. But, for the sake of their own liberty, such advocates must be aware that securing solid, current, thorough, and localized legal advice and training is a necessity for anyone who plans to exercise free-speech rights near abortion clinics.

Quick Counsel for Christians

★ You have a constitutional right to free speech, even when listeners don't want to hear you.

★ The government has, by law, limited your right to free speech near abortion clinics.

★ Laws restricting protests and sidewalk counseling vary from place to place.

★ Many pro-life protesters and sidewalk counselors have been prosecuted, facing steep fines and imprisonment.

★ To protect your liberty, obtain specific legal advice and training <u>before</u> exercising your right to free speech near abortion clinics.